"Dietrich Bonhoeffer is one o[f] twentieth century due to m[a] Nazis and the biographical popularizations of his life and work. In this book, Nicholas Abraham takes us deeper into Bonhoeffer's true contribution to the church: his theology of community. Abraham's ability to write clearly while not sacrificing historical and theological nuance makes this book instantly one of the best introductions to Bonhoeffer's view of 'life together.'"

—**Brandon D. Smith,** assistant professor of theology
and New Testament, Cedarville University;
cofounder of the Center for Baptist Renewal

"Dietrich Bonhoeffer maintained that believers only truly meet each other *through* Christ and *in* Christ. Simply put, there is no Christian community that is more than this, and there is none that is less than this. In *Living Together in Unity with Dietrich Bonhoeffer*, Nicholas Abraham provides a first-class study of Bonhoeffer's thesis and its contemporary significance for the church. Here is an insightful analysis of how God in Christ is present among his followers and, in turn, how these 'communities' of followers assume concrete form in the world."

—**J. Stephen Yuille,** professor of pastoral theology
and spiritual formation, Southwestern Baptist
Theological Seminary, Fort Worth, TX

"Everyone has ideas on what Christian community should be like. And, frankly, some of these ideas should be forgotten forever, while others, like Bonhoeffer's, continue to deserve our attention and contemplation. I'm so thankful for Nick Abraham giving us a beautiful and insightful work on Bonhoeffer's understanding of a truly spiritual Christian community. Read and be ready to live in step with Christ, his people, and the Spirit."

—**Jeff Medders,** author of *Humble Calvinism*

LIVING TOGETHER IN UNITY

WITH

DIETRICH BONHOEFFER

LIVING TOGETHER IN UNITY

WITH

DIETRICH BONHOEFFER

NICHOLAS J. ABRAHAM

LEXHAM PRESS

Living Together in Unity with Dietrich Bonhoeffer
Lived Theology

Lexham Press, 1313 Commercial St., Bellingham, WA 98225
LexhamPress.com

Print ISBN 9781683596691
Digital ISBN 9781683596707
Library of Congress Control Number 2022944257

Series Editor: Michael A. G. Haykin
Lexham Editorial: Todd Hains, Caleb Kormann, Katrina Smith
Cover Design: Sarah Brossow, Brittany Schrock
Typesetting:: Mandi Newell

To my wife Anna:
you are an endless source of encouragement to me,
thank you, I love you.

To my daughter Nora:
I am so proud of the young lady God has made you,
I love you.

And to my son Aden:
I praise God for the promise of the resurrection,
when we will meet face-to-face, I love you.

Contents

Timeline of
Dietrich Bonhoeffer's Life

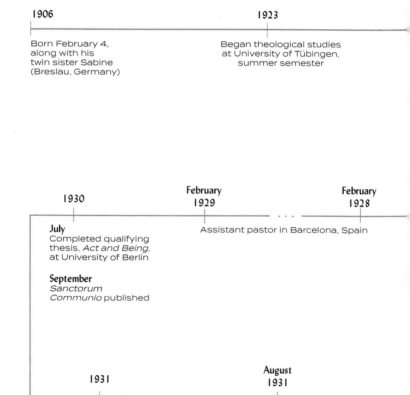

1906

Born February 4,
along with his
twin sister Sabine
(Breslau, Germany)

1923

Began theological studies
at University of Tübingen,
summer semester

1930

July
Completed qualifying
thesis, *Act and Being*,
at University of Berlin

September
*Sanctorum
Communio* published

February
1929

February
1928

Assistant pastor in Barcelona, Spain

1931

Served under Sloan
Fellowship at
Union Theological
Seminary, New York
(academic year)

August
1931

Began post as lecturer
at University of Berlin
(ended summer 1933)

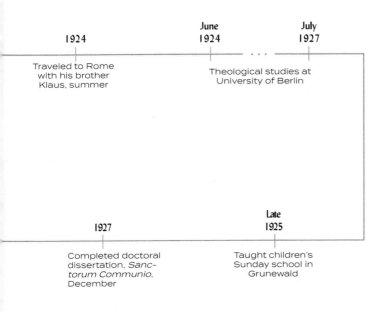

1924

Traveled to Rome with his brother Klaus, summer

June 1924

Theological studies at University of Berlin

July 1927

· · ·

1927

Completed doctoral dissertation, *Sanctorum Communio*, December

Late 1925

Taught children's Sunday school in Grunewald

1931

Served as chaplain at technical college in Charlottenburg

Taught confirmation class in Wedding

November 1931

Ordained into the ministry at St. Matthias Church, Berlin

1932

Lectured on "The Nature of the Church" at University of Berlin, summer semester

1933

Adolf Hitler made chancellor of Germany

Bonhoeffer Began dual pastorate at German Evangelical Church, Sydenham and Reformed Church of St. Paul in London (ended March 10, 1935)

1939

Life Together published

June 2–July 27
Bonhoeffer's second trip to the US

September 1
Germany invaded Poland; England and France declared war on Germany

1939

February
Bonhoeffer had initial contact with political resistance leaders

April
All pastors in Germany required to swear oath of allegiance to Hitler

September–October
Bonhoeffer wrote *Life Together* at his twin sister's former home

November
Kristallnacht (night of broken glass), destruction of synagogues and Jewish-owned shops, 35,000 Jews arrested

1940

Autumn
Bonhoeffer joined the resistance taking a position in the *Abwehr*

1943

January
Bonhoeffer engaged to Maria von Wedemeyer

April 5
Arrested with Hans von Dohnanyi

1934

May 29–31
First meeting
of Confessing
Church in Barmen,
Germany; Barmen
Declaration
adopted

1935

April 26 Bonhoeffer traveled to site
of Confessing Church seminary in
Zingst by the Baltic Sea

June 24 Seminary moved to
Finkenwalde in Pomerania

September 15 Nuremberg Laws
cancel citizenship for German Jews
and prohibit marriage between
Jews and Aryans

December 2 Confessing Church
seminaries and ordinations declared
illegal by the state

1937

October Seminary at
Finkenwalde closed by
Gestapo

November *The Cost of
Discipleship* published

December The Finkenwalde
experience continued in
Köslin and Gross-Schlönwitz,
replacing the seminary

1936

Bonhoeffer no
longer authorized to
teach at University
of Berlin

1944

Held at Tegel
military prison
in Berlin until
October

1945

February
Transferred to
Buchenwald
concentration camp

April 9
Executed at Flossenbürg
concentration camp along
with Hans von Dohnanyi

LIVED
THEOLOGY

Series Preface

Men and women—not ideas—make history. Ideas have influence only if they grip the minds and energize the wills of flesh-and-blood individuals.

This is no less true in the history of Christianity than it is in other spheres of history. For example, the eventual success of Trinitarianism in the fourth century was not simply the triumph of an idea but of the biblical convictions and piety of believers like Hilary and Athanasius, Basil of Caesarea and Macarius-Symeon. Thirteen hundred years later, men and women like William Carey, William Ward, and Hannah Marshman were propelled onto the mission field of India—their grit and gumption founded on the conviction that the living, risen Lord has given his church an ongoing command: "Go therefore and make disciples of all nations, baptizing them in the name of the Father and of the Son and of the Holy Spirit, teaching them to observe all that I have commanded you. And behold, I am with you always, to the end of the age" (Matt 28:19-20 ESV). These verses had an impact when they found a lodging-place in their hearts.

The Lived Theology series traces the way that biblical concepts and ideas are lived out in the lives of Christians, some well known, some relatively unknown (though we hope that more people will know their stories). These books tell the stories of these men and women and also describe the way in which ideas become clothed in concrete decisions and actions.

The goal for all of the books is the same: to remember what lived theology looks like. And in remembering this, we hope that these Christians' responses to their historical contexts and cultures will be a source of wisdom for us today.

And these all, having obtained a good report through faith, received not the promise: God having provided some better thing for us, that they without us should not be made perfect. Wherefore seeing we also are compassed about with so great a cloud of witnesses, let us lay aside every weight, and the sin which doth so easily beset us, and let us run with patience the race that is set before us, Looking unto Jesus the author and finisher of our faith. (Hebrews 11:39–12:2 KVJ)

Michael A. G. Haykin
Chair and Professor of Church History
The Southern Baptist Theological Seminary

Acknowledgments

I am deeply thankful for the help of so many to bring this book to light: Lexham Press, for graciously giving me an opportunity to be published; Todd Hains, for his continual, patient editorial advice and assistance; Rachel Joy Welcher, for her very helpful editorial work; Dave Jones, Ronald Bair, David Greene, and Brenda West, for taking the time to read an early draft and offer feedback; Dr. Stephen Nichols, for his helpful advice on the D.Min. thesis that became this book; Dr. Paul House, for his advice and helpful corrections of an early draft of the book; the Board and congregation of Alpine Bible Church, for giving me freedom to continue my education and write; the congregation of Reformation Bible Church, for their ongoing support; Rev. Dale Boston, for being a good pastor and introducing me to Bonhoeffer; Fred F. Abraham (gidu), who always supported me; Dr. Michael A. G. Haykin, for his friendship, mentorship, and guidance—this book would not exist without his kindness and encouragement; Dr. Joe Harrod, for his support as an additional reader on the D.Min. thesis that became this book; Dr. Coleman Ford, for his early support and guidance at SBTS; Matt Ellington, for being a consistent, encouraging friend and brother; my dear wife Anna, for her relentless encouragement, support, sacrifice, and love, thank you; and my daughter Nora, for patiently enduring my busy school schedule and supporting me. Finally, all thanks, praise, and honor be to God.

Navarre, Ohio
August 28, 2022

CHAPTER 1

What Is Community?

O n Christmas Eve in 1943, Dietrich Bonhoeffer (1906–1945) was alone. He was being held under guard in Tegel military prison in Berlin, Germany. Despite being a pastor and theologian, he was suspected by the Nazi government of involvement with actions against the state. Bonhoeffer, struggling with the disconnection he felt from those he loved, wrote to his dear friend Eberhard Bethge (1909–2000), who was married to Bonhoeffer's niece, Renate Bethge (1925–2019):

> First, there is nothing that can replace the absence of someone dear to us, and one should not even attempt to do so; one must simply persevere and endure it. At first that sounds very hard, but at the same time it is a great comfort, for one remains connected to the other person through the emptiness to the extent it truly remains unfilled. It is wrong to say that God fills the emptiness; God in no way fills it but rather keeps it empty and thus helps us preserve—even if in pain—our authentic communion. Further, the more beautiful and full the memories, the more difficult the separation. But gratitude

transforms the torment of memory into peaceful joy. One
bears what was beautiful in the past not as a thorn but as
a precious gift deep within. One must guard against wal-
lowing in these memories, giving oneself entirely over
to them, just as one does not gaze endlessly at a precious
gift but only at particular times, and otherwise possesses
it only as a hidden treasure of which one is certain. Then
a lasting joy and strength radiate from the past. Further,
times of separation are not lost and fruitless for common
life, or at least not necessarily, but rather in them a quite
remarkably strong communion—despite all problems—
can develop. Moreover, I have experienced especially
here that we can always cope with *facts*; it is only what we
anticipate that is magnified by worry and anxiety beyond
all measure. From first awakening until our return to
sleep, we must commend and entrust the other person
to God wholly and without reserve, and let our worries
become prayer for the other person.[1]

Here we see the raw emotion of separation mixed with a firm
faith in the triune God who is with those who mourn. Bonhoeffer
was not pretending as if he did not feel the pain of being separated from his friends and family. He did not try to spiritualize
away the loneliness or presume God would remove it. Instead,
he saw God's grace amid the ache, knowing that it was proof of
the deep and precious bond he had formed with others.

Bonhoeffer's friend Eberhard had encouraged him to write
prayers in prison that could be distributed to his fellow prisoners for encouragement. A portion of a morning prayer described
Bonhoeffer's faithful stance:

Lord Jesus Christ, you were poor and miserable, impris-
oned and abandoned as I am. You know all human need,

you remain with me when no human being stands by me, you do not forget me and you seek me, you want me to recognize you and turn back to you. Lord, I hear your call and follow. Help me![2]

Bonhoeffer's faith in the Lord Jesus was marked by intense realism. Bonhoeffer increasingly realized the gritty nature of earthly life and he was strengthened by trusting in his Lord who lived an earthly life on his behalf. One might say that Bonhoeffer looked at life, even life as a Christian, realistically. He knew firsthand that life brought about real pain, difficulties, and challenges. During this time in prison, writing letters was a source of comfort and connection. In a letter he wrote to his fiancée, he shared:

You yourself, my parents—all of you, including my friends and students on active service—are my constant companions. Your prayers and kind thoughts, passages from the Bible, long-forgotten conversations, pieces of music, books—all are invested with life and reality as never before. I live in a great unseen realm of whose real existence I'm in no doubt. The old children's song about the angels says "two to cover me, two to wake me," and today we grown-ups are no less in need than children are of preservation, night and morning, by kindly unseen powers.[3]

Even from prison, Bonhoeffer understood the vital importance of community.

WHAT IS COMMUNITY?

What exactly is community? Is it togetherness, fellowship, or camaraderie? Or is it just the absence of being alone? In many ways, a place where we can see the importance of community is in the contemporary church. Many Christians seem to understand the importance of togetherness. Many Christians would affirm the essential nature of Christian community. However, confusion and disagreement abound concerning how to define Christian community. Christian community can be defined as *lifelong fellowship with other believers in Jesus, who won this gift for his people, maintains it by the Holy Spirit and the Word, and ordains it to be best expressed in local churches.* While that definition is loaded with content, much of it is reflected in the apostle Paul's opening greeting to the church in Corinth: "To the church of God that is in Corinth, to those sanctified in Christ Jesus, called to be saints together with all those who in every place call upon the name of our Lord Jesus Christ, both their Lord and ours" (1 Cor 1:2). First, it is a church, the place or really, the people, among whom this fellowship happens. Second, they belong to God. He is the creator of this community. Third, they are sanctified by the Holy Spirit in their belonging to Jesus. The Spirit has set them apart and is conforming them to the image of Jesus. Fourth, the community in Corinth was not disconnected from the broader body of Christ that existed elsewhere. Finally, the community was one marked by ongoing faith in the Lord Jesus. All of these aspects are true today of Christians in community and are thus reflected in the definition above, but having a definition does not ensure a proper operation of community.

Difficulties also arise in describing how Christian community happens or how it is maintained. Often, community in the church today reflects worldly ideas. In the world, people generally prefer to be with other like-minded people doing and valuing the common things of their particular culture. In response to this cultural desire, the world creates opportunities for community so that people with similar purposes and interests can come together. Such community is often valued because of what the members get out of it. Therefore, people believe that the products of community, such as kindness and a sense of belonging, are community itself. Such results of community are not bad in and of themselves. Yet, viewing community as a means to an end—saying that community is about receiving kindness and belonging to something—is an imposition on the true nature of Christian community.

For example, consider the following questions: What is your political affiliation? Do you homeschool? What Bible translation do you use? What do you think about global warming? What kind of entertainment (music, TV, video games) do you enjoy or avoid? Such questions and many more like them can quickly divide people. Groups exist for all kinds of hobbies and special interests. Social media groups are formed around these kinds of issues. People read blogs and listen to podcasts associated with their particular interests and opinions. If you are a homeschool mom who lives in the country and likes dogs, there is probably a group to which you can belong along with a Facebook community you can join. So, is this also true of Christian community? Is community just getting together with people as much like you as possible? Most marketing experts would have you believe that to be the case. Advertising dollars are spent to drive home the message that your new electronic device now grants you access into a particular community of other electronic device owners. So, is this how Christian community should look?

The *Oxford English Dictionary* defines community in one sense as "a group of people who share the same interests, pursuits, or occupation, esp. when distinct from those of the society in which they live."[4] Certainly, we can call groups that form around various causes and interests *community*. The *Oxford English Dictionary* also uses the term "social cohesion" to define community.[5] Social cohesion is probably what most people think about when they think about community. Many might ask, "Do

I click with that person?" Behind such a question is the notion of social cohesion. The kinds of things we have in common with someone is usually the basis for whether we can be in fellowship or in community with that person. We must say that social cohesion is not a bad thing, but any Christian can tell you that social cohesion does not always abound in churches because people are different from one another.

What about when we are placed in contexts where we are encouraged or required to be in community with those with whom we do not share much social cohesion? This happens for most people in various aspects of civic life. On a small scale, people face this in whatever village, town, or city they live. On a grand scale, people face this in their state or province, and, of course, their country. In some sense, we are in community with those with whom we share little to no social cohesion. This may cause us to recede into our more comfortable tribes, avoiding the difficulties of trying to have community with those different from us. The alternative to this approach takes great work, which is to strive toward community with those different from ourselves. The options to either gather with those like us or press on in community with those different from us are placed before all people in the fractured society the contemporary world provides. Differences of opinion and personality are just a part of the challenges we face in Christian community.

As I write this, the world faces a global pandemic due to the COVID-19 virus. The alternatives before us now include an additional challenge—isolation. Loneliness has always been a problem and a challenge to community. However, now much of the world has faced seasons of mandated isolation in order to try to keep one another safe. If we have learned anything from the impact of the COVID-19 crisis on many, it is that it is not good for people to be alone. How can community be built, maintained, or even participated in amid such isolation? Indeed, how can community prevail at all against such challenges?

Differences of opinion and the problem of isolation are no new challenges. God's people have faced these challenges throughout history. The fact that we live in a fallen world has ensured that strife has persisted among people, even God's people. Abram and Lot separated due to strife among their herdsmen (Gen 13). Men like George Whitefield (1714-70) and John Wesley (1703-91) separated over theological convictions. The prophet Elijah faced isolation in his obedience to God's call on his life (1 Kgs 18-19). Martin Luther (1483-1546) stood alone against the failures of the medieval Roman Catholic church to reform itself according to the Scriptures. In our day, we witness a variety of ways to try to face these challenges. It is tempting to listen to how society has sought to deal with differences of opinion and isolation. The cultural response to differences of opinion and isolation ends up in two extremes: fight or flight. People either fight for community by demanding that everyone agree with them, or they take flight, receding into small, like-minded subgroups where their opinions go unchallenged. Neither extreme helps the church recapture true Christian community.

Bringing cultural ideas of community into the church only confuses God's people. Such confusion happens because cultural ideas of community do not rest upon the biblical foundation for Christian community, which is the Lord Jesus. A familiar refrain today is the insightful declaration of John Piper: "God is most glorified in us when we are most satisfied in him."[6] The point of Piper's statement, in part, is to enjoy God for the sake of who he is, not merely because of what one gets from him. The same can be said of Christian community; fellowship with other believers in the body of Christ is to be loved and valued for what it is. Christian community is so lovely because it is community with, through, and in Jesus Christ.

It is not good that man should be alone.

The damage had been done; everything changed. Adam and Eve fled and hid from the Lord as he walked through the garden. Their perfect communion with God was shattered. "But the Lord God called to the man and said to him, 'Where are you?' And he said, 'I heard the sound of you in the garden, and I was afraid, because I was naked, and I hid myself'" (Gen 3:9–10). Adam decided to ignore the problem of which God had earlier warned him—isolation. God had previously said, "It is not good that man should be alone; I will make him a helper fit for him" (Gen 2:18). To be sure, this was at least identifying the way that Adam and Eve would complement one another as image-bearers of the Lord. This complementary union would be codified in their covenant of marriage before God (see Gen 2:24; Matt 19:5–6). Yet, God's statement to Adam was also stating a general principle that *aloneness* is not good. It was *not good* for Adam to be alone. Read through Genesis 1 and 2 and look for things that are labeled *not good*; you will not find many. This is a clue to us of an important fact about how God intends life to function in obedience to him: you are not to be a loner!

Adam's representative fall into sin brought sin and death to all (Rom 5:12ff.). All people *in Adam* were, as the Apostle Paul described, "having no hope and without God in the world" (Eph 2:12). Yet, God acted decisively and sovereignly in his Son. "For while we were still weak, at the right time Christ died for the ungodly" (Rom 5:6). By grace, through faith, as people receive Christ Jesus as their Lord, they are crucified with him, buried, and raised to new life with and in Jesus, who is seated in the heavenly places (see Rom 6:4–8; Eph 2:6). This is the good news of the gospel of Jesus Christ. It is good news for us as individual disciples of Jesus, but also for us *corporately*, as the body of Christ. Together we were crucified with Jesus, we died with Jesus, we were buried with Jesus, we were raised with Jesus, we live with Jesus, and are seated in the heavenly places in Jesus. So, we experience a foundational reality of union with Christ, but that union with Christ is experienced together. Bonhoeffer stated, "Everyone enters discipleship alone, but no one remains alone in discipleship."[7] After all, Jesus prayed for those who would hear and believe in the apostolic testimony "that they may all be one, just as you, Father, are in me, and I in you, that they may also be in us, so that the world may believe that you have sent me" (John 17:21). Union with Christ is the foundation of Christian community.

The church of Jesus Christ is not simply a group of like-minded people gathered around a certain cause or idea. It is not a group of people merely accruing various membership benefits. Such cheap perspectives of community root themselves in shallow theology. These lack the vitality to adequately display the glory of Christ, which is what Christian community is meant to do. Cheap perspectives of community also fail to provide practices that can maintain Christian community, since the community these ideas maintain is deficient. Furthermore, a cheap vision of community cannot attain the very thing for which Jesus prayed for the church, which was union with the Father and the Son. True Christian community must grow from richer theological soil. The production of such soil can come from nowhere else but the Bible. Community in the true church of Jesus Christ roots itself in this soil because the Bible makes clear that Jesus himself is the soil. Thus, the church, the Christian community, is gathered in the name of a person, namely Jesus Christ.

Dietrich Bonhoeffer understood the richness of true Christian community in the face of opposing cultural narratives. In his book *Life Together*, he provided a vision for Christian community that was both biblical and practical. He grasped true community in the church because he lived and exemplified it. His confessional stance concerning Christ and the church rested in God's revelation to his people, namely the Bible. He had what Robert Yarbrough called "confessional courage."[8] As a result, his concept of Christian community was theologically rich and not simply philosophical. He did not rely on cultural norms to drive his vision of community. He showed the importance of relying on God's revelation in the Bible for both the concept and practice of community in the church. Therefore, this book will explore the core biblical themes of Christian community with the help of Bonhoeffer. Before we consider what we will cover, let us first review Bonhoeffer's story.

A PRIVILEGED UPBRINGING

Bonhoeffer was born on February 4, 1906, along with his twin sister Sabine (1906–99). He was the sixth child born to his parents, Karl and Paula Bonhoeffer. At the time of his birth, the family lived in Breslau, Germany. His father, Karl (1868–1948), was a highly regarded professor of psychiatry and neurology.[9] His mother, Paula (1874–1951), presided over the household with a staff of around five, who helped manage the home and assisted in caring for the children. Bonhoeffer had great respect for his parents and remained close to them as he grew.

Bonhoeffer was raised in a privileged environment. He recognized this even at a young age and had once told his sister Susanne (1909–91) he hoped to be able at some point to "live an unsheltered life."[10] He was the son of a successful doctor, part of a large family, and he lived as one would with such a background. Dietrich was the youngest boy of the eight Bonhoeffer children and nearly the youngest child; his little sister Susanne could lay claim to being the baby of the family.[11] This position in birth order shaped a part of his personality as well, essentially being the baby boy of the family. Many have pointed out that this made him nearly destined to take a different route than the rest of his siblings.

Bonhoeffer's path in life is surprising in light of the spiritual ethos of the family. They did not regularly attend church and were rarely involved in a local church at all. Instead of calling on a local parish minister for weddings or funerals, relatives who served in ministry were involved in any type of religious ceremony that was needed within the family. Any Christian influence came from Bonhoeffer's mother, who educated the children in their early years in the home. When she was younger, Paula spent time at Herrnhut, the birthplace of the Moravian Brethren Church. In the history of the church, Herrnhut served as an important place of discipleship and mission for people like John Wesley or the religious community's founder, Nikolaus von Zinzendorf (1700-60). Paula Bonhoeffer retained some of the ideals she learned at Herrnhut, but much of her zeal waned as she grew older. Nevertheless, she taught the children using an illustrated Bible. That style of teaching so impacted Bonhoeffer that when he first began in ministry, he adopted the same style of biblical teaching. He would later employ a similar method of instruction with a rowdy group of inner-city kids that he was preparing for confirmation in 1931 as he told them stories from his time in Harlem and taught them stories from the Bible.[12] Bonhoeffer's personality resembled that of his mother, who enjoyed time with people—unlike his father, who was something of an introvert.[13] Paula's impact in the spiritual area of Bonhoeffer's life was evident. Unfortunately, his father remained mostly uninvolved in the initiating of any spiritual conversations.[14]

Bonhoeffer's twin sister Sabine recalled how at night in their bedrooms they would lie awake talking about eternity and death. They would comfort themselves with hymns they had learned.[15] Sabine wrote, "When at the age of twelve Dietrich got a room of his own, we arranged that he should drum on the wall at night that Susi and I should "think of God." These admonitory bangs happened regularly and became a habit, until Dietrich noticed that they sometimes roused us from our sleep; then he stopped them."[16] As a young man, Dietrich was captivated by spiritual things.

Bonhoeffer's decision to study theology and pursue a career as a theologian came at the young age of thirteen. Though his parents had hoped he would consider a career as a musician due to his talent and love for music, he remained steadfast in his desire to pursue theology. Music could not compare with the excitement he felt from studying theology, like when he read from the theological books owned by his uncle Hans von Hase (1873–1958).[17] His siblings chided him about his decision to pursue a career in an institution like the church and Bonhoeffer replied, "In that case, I shall reform it!"[18] The Bonhoeffer children did not all have the same spiritual leanings as Dietrich did. He was eager to change not only the perspectives of his family toward the church but also the church in Germany itself. Bonhoeffer completed his primary schooling when he was seventeen in the spring of 1923.[19] Later that year, he prepared to begin his university studies and thus start his journey in theology.

FROM PRIVILEGE TO PRISON

Following in the footsteps of his father and brothers, Bonhoeffer enrolled in the University of Tübingen and began his studies there in the fall of 1923. His first semester consisted of primarily philosophy courses, which became a subject embedded in his later writing.[20] After his first term, he went on an extended trip to Rome, Italy with one of his brothers. Upon his return, he immersed himself back into his studies. Toward the end of 1925 he began work on his dissertation, *Sanctorum Communio* (Communion of Saints), which was a study of the social dynamics of the church. It was an interesting choice of study for someone who had not spent a great deal of time in a church up to that point. Nevertheless, he was fascinated with the topic. He spent eighteen months writing, finishing his dissertation in the summer of 1927.[21] His completion of this phase of his education meant that he now needed to serve in his first pastoral role.

Bonhoeffer's pastoral experience began with the Sunday school or confirmation class he taught at a church near the university.[22] By the winter of 1927, he received an offer to assist the pastor of a German-speaking church in Barcelona, Spain. He accepted and worked with the youth there but also had opportunities to preach.[23] Bonhoeffer remained in Barcelona until early 1929. He then returned to Berlin to begin work on his postdoctoral degree. He would complete this work in the spring of 1930, and from this work he would write and later publish *Act and Being*, which was an intense scholarly work dealing with the intersection of philosophy and theology.[24] Bonhoeffer was then offered a yearlong study grant to study and teach at Union Seminary in New York City. He jumped at the opportunity and made important friendships at Union but also in nearby Harlem, where he served at a small African American church.[25]

Again, Bonhoeffer returned to Berlin, this time after his year in New York. He immersed himself in three simultaneous careers: teaching at the University of Berlin, serving for a worldwide ecumenical ministry, and serving as a chaplain to students at the Berlin Technical University.[26] By the winter of 1931, he was officially ordained to the ministry, which helped him in the roles he was occupying.[27] Bonhoeffer later reflected on this time, which lasted through 1933, as an extremely difficult season. This was partly because of the workload but also because of tensions that were rising in Germany as the Nazi party was coming to power. Interestingly, this is also the time that it seems Bonhoeffer was truly converted. He said as much in a letter to a friend as he processed this time of his life.[28] The year 1933 was a pivotal year for Germany and for Bonhoeffer. Hitler and the Nazi party began to take real control, and Bonhoeffer was faced with the decision to act. He spoke and wrote against the Nazi influence in the country and the influence that was infiltrating the church. His speaking and writing would cost him, as the Nazi government did not take criticism lightly. Bonhoeffer was not alone in his stance against the Nazi agenda. A movement called the Confessing Church arose to combat the Nazi influence in the German church. It sought to draft theological statements pushing against the Nazi threat. Bonhoeffer was involved with these statements but became frustrated that they did not go far enough, and he witnessed even some in the Confessing Church caving into Nazi pressure. Discouraged, Bonhoeffer took a pastorate in London in the fall of 1933.[29]

In London, Bonhoeffer pastored two small German-speaking congregations. The Sunday-after-Sunday rhythm of preaching was new to him. However, the crisis in Germany was not wiped from his mind. Though he thought he could perhaps escape the crisis, the church struggle and wider problems in

Germany remained important to him.[30] While in London, he was asked to consider returning to Germany to lead a secretive seminary for the Confessing Church. Things had soured enough in Germany that the Confessing Church had to work secretively in certain things to avoid Nazi conflict. The Confessing Church had broken with the main Nazi-influenced German church and the Confessing Church needed a way to train pastors. Bonhoeffer was tapped as the man for the job.[31] He returned to Germany in the summer of 1935 to lead the seminary that would eventually settle at Finkenwalde. It was there that he lectured on and wrote both *The Cost of Discipleship* and *Life Together*. It was there that he met his friend and later biographer Eberhard Bethge. It was there that Bonhoeffer was galvanized to action in the church struggle he had avoided in London.[32] Unfortunately, the Finkenwalde experience would not last. By direct order of the Nazi government, it was ordered closed in 1937.[33] Bonhoeffer remained in contact with many of his former students after the seminary was disbanded. All Confessing Church pastors were dealt a heavy blow when all German pastors were forced to swear an oath to Hitler in early 1938; unfortunately, many swore this oath.[34]

Eventually, Bonhoeffer's journey in theology would cause him to be faced with deeper challenges as a pastor and as a theologian. He even became a kind of double agent of sorts. Decisions he made amid these challenges would eventually bring about his imprisonment and death. Hans von Dohnanyi (1902–45), Bonhoeffer's brother-in-law, had been trying to bring him into efforts to fight against the Nazi government from within. Dohnanyi worked for the German government and was able to maintain an anti-Nazi stance throughout his time in service.[35] In February 1938, Bonhoeffer's brother Klaus (1901–45) and Hans von Dohnanyi introduced Bonhoeffer to members of a conspiracy within a section of the *Abwehr*, German military intelligence.[36] This meeting set in motion for Bonhoeffer a level of involvement in the fight against the evils of the Nazi government from which he could not return.

Bonhoeffer continued his secretive work with his former seminary students until he decided to take a trip back to the United States in June 1939. The trip resulted from the work of Bonhoeffer's friend Paul Lehmann (1906–94), whom he had met on his first trip to the United States. The Nazis had already carried out the atrocities of *Kristallnacht*, murdering and arresting thousands of Jews. Bonhoeffer was planning to refuse the upcoming draft to the military, which his American friends knew would mean death for him. Therefore, Bonhoeffer was brought to the United States through the German refugee program as both an itinerant preacher and a visiting professor. This visit to the United States did not conjure up the same positive feelings that his first trip had in 1930 and 1931.[37] Nearly as soon as he arrived he began to struggle with why he was even there.

In a letter to Paul Lehmann in late June, he explained that he would be going back to Germany in August or even late July: "I am enjoying a few weeks in freedom, but on the other hand, I feel, I must go back to the "trenches" (I mean the Church-struggle)."[38] One biographer of Bonhoeffer explained that his time in the United States for those six weeks forged a new resolve in Bonhoeffer.[39] He was ready to go home and act. By the autumn of 1940, he had made up his mind to join the resistance.[40] His official acceptance into the *Abwehr* took time. Meanwhile, he was under investigation by the Reich Central Security Office for his preaching and teaching.[41] Despite these investigations and all of his efforts in the Confessing Church, he was finally accepted into the *Abwehr* in October 1940, exempting him from military service.[42] His life became even more complex.

Despite being accepted by the *Abwehr*, he was still under suspicion for actions subverting the people. He was not granted acceptance into the Reich Writer's Guild in November 1940, which effectively kept him from public writing.[43] However, this did not keep him from actually writing. During the winter of 1940 through 1941, he spent three months in the village of Ettal across the street from the Benedictine monastery and in the monastery itself. While there, he began work on his final major work, *Ethics*, which he was not able to finish. At the monastery, he was able to discuss his books *The Cost of Discipleship* and *Life Together*, from which the monks read aloud during mealtimes.[44] Outside of his time at the monastery, this period of his life was multifaceted. He carried on as a pastor. He stayed in contact with Confessing Church pastors and their families. He operated essentially as a double agent within the *Abwehr*. Additionally, he stayed in contact with his contacts outside of the country.[45]

The complex life Bonhoeffer lived during these years was hard for some to understand, specifically those with whom he could not share all the details. A friend and mentor of Bonhoeffer's, Karl Barth (1886–1968), grew suspicious of him when he heard of his involvement with the *Abwehr*, which changed their relationship. Others had the same concerns, but it seems that Bonhoeffer was unaware of the impressions he was leaving.[46] However, he had positive aspects of his life at the time. He had developed a relationship with Maria von Wedemeyer (1924–77). The relationship brought him great joy; it was a joy that he had been without thus far in his life. The two were engaged in January 1943. Wedemeyer informed Bonhoeffer of her decision by letter.[47] However, the serious nature of his involvement in conspiracy came to a head when he was arrested along with Hans von Dohnanyi on April 5, 1943.[48]

Bonhoeffer was first put in Tegel military prison in Berlin. He was able to have visitors at Tegel, frequently seeing Maria and his parents. However, as things worsened, he lost his privileges.[49] He remained at Tegel through October 1944.[50] Earlier in 1944, Bonhoeffer wrote to his friend Eberhard: "At eight this morning I heard, as a fine beginning for the day, a chorale prelude on *"Was Gott tut, das ist wohlgetan"* [Whatever God Ordains Is Right]; I listened to it with thoughts of you and my godchild! I hadn't heard an organ for a long time, and its sound was like a fortress in time of trouble."[51] Sitting in his prison cell, Bonhoeffer was able to hear the music coming from a nearby church. The hymn was a fitting one for his situation. It was a hymn that recognizes the sovereignty and providence of God and affirms that everything this sovereign God does is right. Even in Bonhoeffer's dire situation, God was good and was doing what was right. What an important reminder for Bonhoeffer as he reflected on the times gone by, thinking on time with his friends and family, as well as times with the Christian community. At that point, he could only reflect on the blessings of the community he had previously experienced. Hearing the hymn redirected his thoughts on the Lord of the Christian community. Bonhoeffer found hope amid darkness.

CONCLUSION

In the darkness that assails the contemporary church, a fresh, biblical vision is needed for community that is not driven by cultural norms. Such a vision will redirect us to the light of Christ in the challenges we face. I contend that in his work *Life Together* and much of his other writing, Bonhoeffer provided that biblical vision of Christian community. Whether you are a pastor, church leader, church member, frustrated church attender, or even unsure about Jesus, Christian community is something worth your time and thought. This book explains Bonhoeffer's view of community and argues that it must be retrieved for the contemporary church. Bonhoeffer showed how Christian community is created and maintained not through fanciful or clever techniques, but in Christ through the ordinary means of grace and the spiritual disciplines. In *Life Together* and his other writings, he provided a timeless theological vision of community that finds its center in Christ. Therefore, this work retrieves a lost but important theology and methodology of community.

This book will continue to explore aspects of Bonhoeffer's life as we engage with his writing to recover the heart of Christian community. Considering Bonhoeffer's story is important because he lived what he believed and often grew in what he believed as he lived. As we continue to grow in our relationship with Christ, we experience this same pattern of growth. This book will provide summaries and considerable interaction with Bonhoeffer's key writings on the subject, like *Life Together*, focusing on the core themes and ideas that Bonhoeffer developed. In chapter 2, we will consider the theme of Christ and the church by exploring this vital component of the Christian faith. The relationship between Christ and the church is the backbone of Christian community. Chapters 3 through 6 will develop core theological themes regarding community found in Bonhoeffer's writing.

Christian community is through and in Jesus Christ (chapter 3).

Both of the prepositions in the statement above are incredibly important: *through* and *in*. Christian community is *through* Jesus because he is the means by which it exists. It is *in* Jesus because he is the means by which it is sustained. Anything less than this is not Christian. Community for the sake of itself, without dependence on Jesus and faith in Jesus, cannot be Christian community.

Community can have many foundations in society. People gather around ideas, causes, or shared interests. This is not what Christian community is—at least not as Bonhoeffer sees it. It would even be reductionistic to say that Christian community is all about a person. In a sense, Christian community is about the person of Jesus Christ, but his use of *through* and *in* keeps Christian community from merely being *about* Jesus. For Bonhoeffer, there is something far deeper going on in Christian community than simply being a Jesus fan club. Christians gathered in community are seeking to grow in relationship with Jesus, not merely learn about him.

Christian community is a divine reality, not an ideal (chapter 4).

For God, who is outside of time, Christian community already exists. Such an idea is foundational to the relationship between Christ and the church. "The Lord knows who are his" (2 Tim 2:19). We do not seek Christian community as though it were something Christians create. Such an idea flies in the face of merely thinking about how to *do* church. Instead, being *in* Christ makes us part of the Christian community, part of the church. Therefore, we should seek to live out what is already intently real to God. One might think about the biblical themes of shadows or copies of heavenly realities existing here on earth (see Col 2:17; Heb 8:5, 10:1). While churches may have an earthly feel to them and a flesh and blood existence in time, the church of Jesus Christ is a heavenly reality. An understanding of this heavenly reality should be evident in the regular life of a Christian community.

Christian community is spiritual, not emotional[52] (chapter 5).

Conflict arises among Christian communities when personal preferences begin to rule the day. The church has always faced this; Bonhoeffer faced this within a country grappling with abuses of power from the Nazi government and divisions over allegiances. Some of the fallout among Bonhoeffer's contemporaries was to form church as people thought it should be or felt it should be. Instead, Bonhoeffer argued for an understanding of Christian community that is spiritual or controlled by the Holy Spirit rather than by people's emotions and preferences. Bonhoeffer fought against emotional decision-making on a broad scale with the Nazis' control of the church in Germany, but also on a small scale with the individual opinions of those he knew and worked with in the church.

For many people, things are done or decisions are made based on how they feel. Yet relying on feeling could be a way to *not* rely on the Spirit, who is to guide the Christian community. What binds together the community and keeps it moving forward is the God who is spirit, not emotional beings who are flesh. This is not to diminish the value of feelings, but simply to test them by the ministry of the Spirit in the Word.

Christian community is in and of the Word (chapter 6).

Just as the Word became immensely important to Bonhoeffer, so should the Word be continually central to the Christian community. One might say that the way by which God ensures that Christian community is *through* and *in* Jesus is to have it be *in* and *of* the Word. The Scriptures are how the Word, namely

Jesus, is made known to the Christian community. Therefore, the Scriptures must be central to the Christian community.

This theme has a close connection to the previous, in that both the Spirit and the Word are confessing that God's voice and leadership must be supreme in the Christian community. To be sure, all the themes come together, since the Lord is one. The Lord Jesus Christ, through his Word and his Spirit, brings his church into being, uniting his people to himself for love and service.

As we work through these themes, we will see that Bonhoeffer's insights are the culmination of his deep, theological thinking married with real life. You will notice that chapters 2–4 will deal with core theological concepts that really serve as a foundation for understanding Christian community. Chapters 5–7, while continuing to reflect on these theological concepts, will conclude our study by discussing practical ways we can build upon these foundations.

CHAPTER 2

Christ and the Church

"**F**or the first time, I came to the Bible. That, too, is an awful thing to say. I had often preached, I had seen a great deal of the church, had spoken and written about it—and yet I was not yet a Christian but rather in an utterly wild and uncontrolled fashion my own master."[1] In Bonhoeffer's testimony of his conversion to faith in Jesus, he described great changes in his life in the early 1930s. He had been trying to balance three simultaneous jobs. His confession about having been in ministry and yet not being converted pointed to a struggle he faced during this time. Bonhoeffer wrestled between the two vocations of academic work and local church ministry. Initially opting more for the former, he began to be increasingly drawn to the latter. Bonhoeffer went into more detail in his testimony:

> I know that at that time I turned the doctrine of Jesus Christ into something of personal advantage for myself. ... I pray to God that will never happen again. Also I had never prayed, or prayed only very little. For all my loneliness, I was quite pleased with myself. Then the Bible, and in particular the Sermon on the Mount, freed me from that. Since then everything has changed. I have felt

this plainly, and so have other people about me. It was a
great liberation. It became clear to me that the life of a
servant of Jesus Christ must belong to the church, and
step by step it became clearer to me how far that must go.[2]

His participation in Christian community alongside others
in a local church was a key component of this shift in his life.
Bonhoeffer had tasted this in Barcelona, in London, and certainly
later in New York, specifically in the church in Harlem. This
struggle between vocations was the means by which Bonhoeffer
came to understand the inseparable value and importance of
Christ and the church. He recognized that Christian community,
which he grew to love as he grew in his faith, was constituted
by the relationship of Christ to his church.

THE CHRISTIAN COMMUNITY

Many authors say that they come to understand a subject
by writing about it. In a way, this happened for Bonhoeffer.
Bonhoeffer's appreciation for and understanding of Christian
community culminated in his book *Life Together*. Bonhoeffer
began *Life Together* by quoting one of David's praises of community in the book of Psalms: "How very good and pleasant it is
when kindred live together in unity" (Ps 133:1 NRSV). This verse
captures the way that Bonhoeffer viewed community: he saw it
as truly good and pleasant. Apart from simply quoting a verse,
he set out to look at how the Scriptures can provide direction
for "life together under the Word."[3] Bonhoeffer described the
privilege that Christian community is—particularly living with
other Christians. He declared, "visible community is grace."[4] As
a stark contrast to the grace of Christian community experienced by believers, Jesus dwelt with enemies. This was true for
him to the point of death on the cross. Therefore, those following

Christ share in the same scenario he experienced, namely living among enemies or unbelievers. This encapsulates the purpose for Christians, that they live among unbelievers to proclaim and serve Christ. Jesus' followers find themselves spread across the earth waiting for the day when they will be drawn together in him.[5] Bonhoeffer declared, "Until then, God's people remain scattered, held together in Jesus Christ alone, having become one because they remember *him* in the distant lands, spread out among the unbelievers."[6]

During this time of waiting for Jesus to consummate his kingdom, Christian community anticipates the coming kingdom. Not all who follow Jesus are able to experience the grace of community. Yet, as Bonhoeffer explained concerning the apostle John in Revelation 1, even the lonely and exiled are comforted by their inclusion in the heavenly community in the Spirit, by the Word. Nevertheless, having other Christians around gives life and encouragement. As biblical examples of such encouraging relationships, Bonhoeffer referred to Paul's relationship with Timothy or the way the apostle John addressed those to whom he wrote his epistles.[7]

One could say that typical Christian experience brings about a desire for company with brothers and sisters. Bonhoeffer reassured, "The believer need not feel any shame when yearning for the physical presence of other Christians, as if one were still living too much in the flesh."[8] He made this point by beginning with creation. God made humans with bodies. The Lord Jesus came in a body, suffered in a body, and was raised in a body. Bonhoeffer pointed to the receiving of Jesus in the body in the Lord's Supper. Finally, believers will be resurrected in a body. Bonhoeffer wanted to make plain that the Lord affirms physical fellowship among believers as displayed in creation, the coming of Jesus as the God-man, and the surety of the resurrection for believers. Thus, Christians praise the triune God for the bodily presence of another believer. For Bonhoeffer, the presence of Christ is mediated through the presence of another believer.[9] This was a central part of Bonhoeffer's theology.

As much as community is to be a normal aspect of a Christian's life, Bonhoeffer acknowledged that believers' experience community can vary. "Therefore, let those who until now have had the privilege of living a Christian life together with other Christians praise God's grace from the bottom of their hearts."[10] The fact is that Christian community is a gift. The need to give thanks and to understand the variations of community among Christians only exemplifies the fact that it is a gift. Yet, Bonhoeffer explained that the desire for community is inherent in every believer.[11]

In his book *Life Together*, Bonhoeffer often preferred to call an assembly of Christians a Christian community, not a church. While that may seem like an unnecessary distinction to make, it is important for understanding Bonhoeffer's philosophy of community for a couple of reasons. First, Bonhoeffer wrote *Life Together* after having lived with the seminary students he led. His seminary was a Christian community, which is why *Life Together* serves as a helpful text for groups other than a local church. Second, Bonhoeffer states in his preface that *Life Together* was written for the church.[12] Those in Christian communities outside of the church need to be connected to local churches because Christ's call is to himself and to his church. Furthermore, Bonhoeffer wanted to show the church that it needed to behave more like a Christian community. He grappled with this in real experience. Bonhoeffer learned this on the job as it were.

Bonhoeffer's first official church position came some years before the events of *Life Together* in early 1928 as he received a call the year before inviting him to come to Barcelona, Spain to serve as an assistant pastor.[13] He would be confronted by the idea of the Christian community he would later write about.

FIRST PASTORATE IN BARCELONA

Bonhoeffer finally arrived in Barcelona in mid-February 1928, after a week's vacation in Paris.[14] This was much later than the pastor he was serving under, Fritz Olbricht, would have liked. Olbricht was in desperate need of help. And Bonhoeffer's tardiness, about three months late, caused the cancellation of some services at the Barcelona church. One biographer noted, "Bonhoeffer believed Olbricht had missed his true calling, 'He would have been better suited as a forest ranger or an infantryman,' Dietrich told his mother."[15] The young Bonhoeffer, though quite brilliant, was not without his opinions or his rather harsh way of looking at things. Furthermore, what is fascinating about Bonhoeffer winding up in a pastoral role is his lack of real experience with the church. Yet, it seems he had a fascination with the concept of church. That interest developed into his early doctoral work. What was missing from the young Bonhoeffer's interests was Jesus. He had much to say about Jesus' church but had not yet taken hold of Christ by faith. Yet, while Bonhoeffer served in churches, starting in Barcelona, he met Jesus in the Scriptures.

The church in Barcelona ministered primarily to German expatriates. His primary responsibilities in the church were in the children's ministry and the high school youth group. In addition, he taught a few classes at the German school. He also shared in the pulpit ministry of the church. He saw the youth group grow from one to fifteen after a few weeks. Bonhoeffer also connected well with the adults of the congregation and was frequently invited into their homes and joined them on evenings out. People were attending and responding to Bonhoeffer's sermons in a greater proportion than to those of the tired pastor of the congregation, which caused some friction between the two.[16] Nevertheless, Bonhoeffer was invited in November 1928 to stay on as assistant pastor in Barcelona, but he declined. Bonhoeffer remained unsure at that point whether his long-term calling was in an academic setting or in the pastorate. The pastorate would require attending a preacher's seminary, which he saw as unneeded at that time. Instead, he decided to pursue a post-doctoral degree.[17] Bonhoeffer's struggle between academic and pastoral vocations continued, showing up again as he served in a pastorate some years later in London.

LONDON: A TIME OF DECISION

Bonhoeffer's home in London was infested with mice, and he was frequently ill due to the change in climate and the large, drafty Victorian home that served as his parsonage.[18] The zealous young man who wanted a career in theology was now having to lead others in the theology he was coming to understand. The privileged boy who had not grown up in church was tasked with the responsibility of caring for two congregations and preaching every Sunday. All the while, his mind was still on the struggle in his homeland. He had not totally abandoned the church struggle in Germany, but his friend Eberhard said that "what he wanted was a period of seeking and testing in a small, quiet congregation."[19]

While Bonhoeffer was in London, the Confessing Church met in May 1934 for three days to formulate a theological statement known as the "Barmen Declaration." This came as the Confessing Church needed to take a stand against the rising Nazi influence in the German churches.[20] The meeting, referred to as a synod, forged a clear break from the Nazi-controlled church. Of this meeting, one Bonhoeffer biographer stated, "the Synod declared its loyalty to the fundamental teachings of Martin Luther, with his threefold 'solus': *solus Christus, sola scriptura and sola fide* [Christ alone, Scripture alone and Faith alone]."[21] The Barmen Declaration sparked many things, but the most significant for Bonhoeffer was the creation of the Confessing Church seminaries. In March 1934, the Old Prussian preachers' seminaries were shut down due to an infiltration of Nazi ideology. Those in the Confessing Church needed to find a new means of ordination that reflected their beliefs and practices, as they increasingly could not rely on anything related to the Nazi-controlled church. At the beginning of the summer of 1934, Bonhoeffer was approached to be a part of these seminaries. The decision hung in the balance for him for quite some time, likely due to his temporary withdrawal from Germany, and it would be nearly a year until he would begin work in one of these seminaries.[22] Unfortunately, the final declaration drawn up by the synod lacked the initial strength the first draft had. Participating at a distance in London, Bonhoeffer was discouraged by the failure of the Confessing Church in Germany to draw up a confession of faith that adequately opposed the Nazi influence in the churches.

Despite his disappointment, Bonhoeffer's growth in his pastoral role continued. In the summer of 1934, he preached a baptism sermon from a well-known Old Testament text. His text for that day was from the book of Joshua: "And if it is evil in your eyes to serve the Lord, choose this day whom you will serve, whether the gods your fathers served in the region beyond the River, or the gods of the Amorites in whose land you dwell. But as for me and my house, we will serve the Lord" (Josh 24:15). Bonhoeffer fashioned this verse into a comfort and challenge for a child being baptized and her family:

From now on, your house shall have only one Lord, Jesus Christ, only one will, the will of God, only one spirit, the Holy Spirit. There is no room left for selfishness and egoism—for, [as] for me and my house we will serve the Lord. There would be something wrong with this day if there would not be a real change in your homelife from now on. For Jesus has come to dwell with you and wherever Jesus comes he changes lives and houses.[23]

The words Pastor Bonhoeffer spoke gave a clear charge of discipleship to Jesus Christ. Bonhoeffer now called others to the same life to which he had been called. While he called the child's family to a changed life amid their discipleship with the Lord, Bonhoeffer was living something about which he would later write. At the beginning of his other well-known book, *The Cost of Discipleship*, he developed the idea of "cheap grace," which was another way of describing a misunderstanding of God's grace. At one point, Bonhoeffer described cheap grace as "baptism without the discipline of community."[24] He was making a similar statement in his sermon in London, which was that community is a Christian discipline. Just as he called the church to the discipline of Christian living in their homes and among the church, so Bonhoeffer was experiencing his own discipline of community serving as the pastor. God, it seems, was teaching the young pastor on the job.

Though he had been involved in the academic study of theology and church ministry before his time in London, he now came to Scripture in a way that he had not before; he came to know Jesus in a way that he had not before. Bonhoeffer would say, "It became clear to me that the life of a servant of Jesus Christ must belong to the church, and step-by-step it became clearer to me how far it must go."[25] Part of his new relationship to the Bible came from the practical commands of passages like the Sermon on the Mount (Matt 5–7), resulting in a new life for Bonhoeffer. This new life was to be, as he later wrote to his brother, "a life of uncompromising discipleship, following Christ according to the Sermon on the Mount."[26] He understood the call that Jesus had placed on his life: a call heard through and in the Scriptures. Bonhoeffer's relationship to the Word became an increasingly prominent theme that gripped his writing and ministry, particularly in *The Cost of Discipleship*. In other words, Bonhoeffer began to see that the Scriptures were for him, and in them God was calling him to obey. Bonhoeffer also grasped his call to the people of London; this same call would soon bring him back to his people in Germany.

CAUGHT UP IN GOD'S PROVIDENCE

The biblical book of Esther portrays a similar picture of God's providence working in an individual's life. Like Esther, Bonhoeffer seems to have been in the right place at the right time. Yet, the Lord wants us to see that it is he who orchestrated the events of Esther's life for his own purposes. When the Jewish people were threatened in the story of the book of Esther, it seems that only Queen Esther could step in. Due to a conflict between the king's chief official, Haman, and Mordecai, Haman set out to have the Jews in the kingdom destroyed as an extreme act of vengeance against Mordecai. Yet Mordecai's niece, Esther, had providentially become queen. She was reminded by her uncle Mordecai, "Who knows whether you have not come to the kingdom for such a time as this?" (Esth 4:14). Esther was in a position to act courageously and obey the Lord.

Similarly, Bonhoeffer had retreated to London to serve the Lord away from the church struggle, yet the struggle found Bonhoeffer and a need presented itself for which this budding pastor-theologian had been made, which was to return to Germany to lead the Confessing Church seminary. Esther did not know all that God was doing through and around her, yet God was working. Bonhoeffer did not know the God he once studied, yet that same God was at work in his life.

Only God could take someone from a background like Bonhoeffer's and make him a servant in and for the church. Bonhoeffer began to understand how the apostle Paul referred to the church as "those sanctified in Christ Jesus, called to be saints together with all those who in every place call upon the name of our Lord Jesus Christ, both their Lord and ours" (1 Cor 1:2). As a follower of Jesus, Bonhoeffer was called together with all who likewise called on the name of Jesus. Bonhoeffer would state elsewhere that Jesus's call to obey him was a call to community with Jesus.[27] In other words, as people obey and follow Jesus by grace through faith, they become part of the community of Jesus, the Christian community—the church.

Bonhoeffer was no longer simply caught up in the study of the church as an organization or a social society. This, in summary, is how he thought of the church as a young doctoral student. Instead, Bonhoeffer had now become enthralled by the Lord of this church. He later acknowledged that it was through the cross, through Jesus's work on the cross, that people came into community with Jesus and thereby other Christians.[28] Things began to come together, to overlap. Bonhoeffer's academic training and his growing fascination with and love for the church had coalesced in his new love for Jesus. It was the Lord Jesus who had sought him, bought him, and taught him. As he grew in his faith in the years following his time in London, he had an ongoing exchange with one of his mentors, Karl Barth. Barth basically separated rigorous theological study from spiritual practices of devotion; he could not see them as being connected or as serving one another. Bonhoeffer disagreed and had begun to see how those two things could come together. In a letter, he wrote to Barth: "The questions young theologians are seriously asking us today are: How can I learn to pray? How can I learn to read Scripture? If we do not help them with these questions, we are not helping them at all. ... It is perfectly clear to me that none of these things has any legitimacy if not accompanied—simultaneously!—by genuinely serious, rigorous theological, exegetical, and dogmatic work."[29] What Bonhoeffer was declaring was that Christ and the church are best understood when a serious study of the Scriptures is paired with a serious devotion to God. These two worlds are not at odds with one another and what a delightful discovery that must have been for Bonhoeffer. He was able to bring these different worlds together within himself to serve his new Lord. In his statement to Barth, he revealed a willingness to bring his two passions together. This is what he did in the seminary he was charged to lead. This is what he did in *Life Together*. This was Bonhoeffer seeing the correlation of Christ and the church.

A CHRIST-CENTERED UNITY

One aspect of Bonhoeffer's work consisted of involvement with the broad ecumenical movement, which was an attempt to bring Christians together from across the world toward some kind of unity. He traveled for conferences and made contacts with a number of different individuals through this work. The relationships he developed served as contacts for his later involvement with the *Abwehr* mentioned in the first chapter. In a letter to one of his English contacts in the summer of 1935, Bonhoeffer expressed his reasons for participating in the ecumenical work:

"Can there be anything finer and more promising to a Christian pastor and teacher than to co-operate in the preparation for a great oecumenical synod which views the final task of hearing the Word of our Lord Jesus Christ together; of being obedient in the faith of the wonder-working power of the Holy Spirit; and of praying, even in this world, for a visible unification of disrupted Christendom?"[30] Notice his main goals: hearing the Word together, obedience in the faith by the power of the Holy Spirit, and prayer.

Some hear about ecumenical work and cringe. Unfortunately, ecumenism in the history of the church has, at times, led to a diminished view of the gospel, the Scriptures, and God himself. Bonhoeffer himself later spoke of the potential dangers of the ecumenical movement in an essay: "[it] is either obedience to the promise of Jesus Christ that there be one flock and one shepherd, or it is the reign of false peace and false unity constructed on the lie of the devil in the guise of an angel."[31] Considering these dangers, Bonhoeffer had his reasons for involving himself with ecumenical work and as he stated them [hearing the Word together, obedience in the faith by the power of the Holy Spirit, and prayer], one finds little with which to argue. One scholar has noted, "Lutherans' participation in ecumenical dialogues has been coterminous with their growing awareness as a global movement."[32] While this may be true of the larger Lutheran movement of which Bonhoeffer was a part, he had his own reasons for his involvement. His reasons were not so weak that they could be discarded for the sake of unity with others that did not affirm his theological reasons. In the same letter to an English contact, Bonhoeffer made plain that he could not join in an ecumenical dialogue that allowed the German Christians ruled by the Nazi government to also have a seat at the table. Bonhoeffer declared,

I am writing all this as a member of the Confessional Church in Germany. At the same time I must state that, with regard to the German Reich Church [which was controlled by the Nazi party], the position of my Church is fundamentally different from its attitude towards all other Churches of the world, as the Confessional Evangelical Church in Germany disclaims and wholly contradicts the Reich Church to accept our Lord Jesus Christ as God and Saviour. There may be [some] ... of the Reich Church ... who propound a theology which is to be called a Christian theology. ... But the teaching as well as the action of the responsible leaders of the Reich Church has clearly proved that this church does no longer serve Christ but that it serves the Antichrist.[33]

The point for Bonhoeffer was that, in the quest for unity, there are lines that cannot be crossed—namely, a clear, biblical confession of faith in the Lord Jesus Christ *and* a life of actions that display such faith. For Bonhoeffer, both one's teaching and one's action must be orthodox. Bonhoeffer saw neither displayed in the Nazi-controlled church of his day and, therefore, it was impossible to have unity with such a church.

Bonhoeffer has much to teach us in both his willingness to take part in ecumenical work as well as his unwillingness to sacrifice right belief and right practice. Such tension explains Bonhoeffer. It also explains why so many can get him wrong. Many do not like tension, and thus, many cast off Bonhoeffer in favor of one of the two extremes—either sacrificing everything for unity or disdaining unity for the cause of being right. The fact is, Bonhoeffer was committed to the Lord Jesus, and, for him, this informed every aspect of life. For Bonhoeffer, to be a Christian carried with it a certain *oughtness*. He declared that elements such as hearing the Word together, obedience in the faith by the power of the Holy Spirit, and prayer *ought* to be part of every Christian's life in the church. Yet he desired, as the Lord Jesus prayed, for the church to be one. This desire came from his understanding of the unity of Christians with Christ. Christ and the church *are* one, therefore, it would follow that they should look like it.

CHRIST AND THE CHURCH IN *LIFE TOGETHER*

When his time in London came to a close, Bonhoeffer would soon be back in Germany leading the Confessing Church seminary he was asked about. During his time as director of the seminary, he taught through and lived the key themes prevalent in *Life Together*: Christian community is about Christ and the church; Christian community is through and in Jesus Christ; Christian community is a divine reality and not an ideal; Christian community is spiritual and not emotional; Christian community is in and of the Word. These themes are important for understanding Bonhoeffer the man because he lived for Christ and the church.

CONCLUSION

Jesus and the church became increasingly central themes in Bonhoeffer's life and ministry. His conversion through the Scriptures had a profound impact on his views of these foundational aspects of the faith. Not only did Bonhoeffer's personal beliefs change and not only was he taken down from being the master of his own life, but he was thrust into situations wherein he needed to shepherd people in what he was coming to believe. It seems that Bonhoeffer essentially learned how to be a pastor while pastoring. Nevertheless, God had his own plans for Bonhoeffer, and Bonhoeffer's own words would become somewhat prophetic: "We must be ready to allow ourselves to be interrupted by God, who will thwart our plans and frustrate our ways time and again."[34] The Lord used Bonhoeffer's plans to study the church as an academic exercise to merge serious study with practical devotion. This was how he came to truly understand Christ and his church. Bonhoeffer had grown to know the God who had sovereignly brought him into the Christian community.

CHAPTER 3

Community through and in Jesus

At the beginning of 1924, just before his eighteenth birth-day, Bonhoeffer hurt himself ice skating. The fall was enough to leave him unconscious for a short while. This was enough of a scare for his parents to come and visit him at university.[1] Like his fathers and brothers before him, Bonhoeffer had enrolled in the University of Tübingen. He had begun his studies there in the fall of 1923.[2] His first term was already behind him and he was anticipating spending his spring term elsewhere. It was at the time of his ice-skating accident that he was preparing to spend the spring term in Rome with his brother Klaus who had just passed his bar examinations. Bonhoeffer's time in Rome would end up becoming one of the most memorable periods of his life.[3]

Rome fascinated Bonhoeffer, partly because of the frequent trips many of his family members had taken there in years past. He was deeply interested in ancient Rome yet knew little about the modern city. He rarely kept a diary throughout his life but did so during his time in Rome. He met a young priest from Bologna on his way there, with whom he conversed often during his stay about the practices and beliefs of the Roman Catholic Church. Being a Lutheran, though not previously highly devoted to his church, Bonhoeffer knew very little about the Catholic church.[4] Eberhard Bethge, Bonhoeffer's close friend and biographer, noted that this trip had a great impact on Bonhoeffer's interpretation of the Roman Catholic Church.[5] What Bonhoeffer experienced in Rome also began to shape his views on the church and faith, views that would change his life in the years to come. He began to get a taste of the fellowship or communion of saints, which is central to the understanding of church, whether Catholic or Protestant.

Bonhoeffer returned home to Berlin from Rome and immediately immersed himself into the life of university studies. Bethge noted, "His journey to Rome essentially helped him to articulate the theme of 'the church.'"[6] He would begin to sort through this theme more in just a year after his return from Rome as he began his dissertation, which was remarkable for him to be writing at the young age of nineteen.[7] In that year, he studied under well-known professors of the German theological world, such as Adolf von Harnack (1851–1930), who was a close neighbor of the Bonhoeffers as well as the director of the theological faculty at Berlin University.[8] Another of his professors, Karl Holl (1866–1926), was a renowned Luther scholar whom one biographer claims shaped Bonhoeffer's view of Martin Luther more than anyone else.[9] A third professor was Reinhold Seeberg (1859–1935), who went on to supervise Bonhoeffer's dissertation.[10] These scholars impacted Bonhoeffer, but he soon began to chart his own path.

Towards the end of 1925, he began work on his dissertation, *Sanctorum Communio*. He spent eighteen months writing and finished in the summer of 1927. In his dissertation, Bonhoeffer would grapple with important theological concepts regarding how people in the church interacted with one another, yet he was missing clear faith in Jesus. His later conversion and growth in grace would help him to articulate that the church existed and was maintained through and in Jesus, not through sociological elements.

FOUNDATIONS IN *SANCTORUM COMMUNIO*

A theologian must start somewhere. For Bonhoeffer, that beginning was with his work on *Sanctorum Communio*. One scholar stated that Bonhoeffer's theology cannot be properly understood without having a grasp of *Sanctorum Communio*.[11] Such a statement displays the profound importance of this work. Bonhoeffer thought that his perspective in *Sanctorum Communio* was a third way to approach the church distinguishing him from both Karl Barth and leading thinkers in the field of sociology.[12] He borrowed and refashioned a concept from German philosopher Georg W. F. Hegel (1770–1831), changing Hegel's statement "God existing as community" to "Christ existing as church-community."[13] This hinted at the theological direction he increasingly took over the course of his life, namely that Christology was the theological center of the church. In other words, he saw the study of Christ as the most important aspect of theology.

Of his methodology in *Sanctorum Communio*, Bonhoeffer noted, "In this study social philosophy and sociology are employed in the service of theology. Only through such an approach, it appears, can we gain a systematic understanding of the community-structure of the Christian church."[14] We can see Bonhoeffer's approach, attempting to bring together the worlds of social philosophy, sociology, and theology in his dissertation. One biographer noted of Bonhoeffer's work in *Sanctorum Communio* that it sparked much criticism, because scholars from all three of these worlds had their disagreements with Bonhoeffer's attempt to synthesize them.[15] Such was Bonhoeffer's frequent approach, to forge a new path.

Bonhoeffer's supervisor for the dissertation, Reinhold Seeberg, summarized his student's achievement and promise:

> The author is not only well oriented in the discipline of theology, but also has worked his way intelligently into the field of sociology. He clearly possesses a great gift for systematic thinking, as demonstrated by the dialectics in the structure of his thesis as a whole, and in its detail. He is concerned to find his way independently, and is always prepared to offer skillful counter-arguments to the opinions of others. Even though one might not always be able to concur with his judgments, one will readily recognize the scholar's interest and the energy of his argumentation.[16]

Bonhoeffer's independent thought is very evident not only in *Sanctorum Communio* but also in other theological views he later developed. Commonly, Bonhoeffer is either associated with the work and beliefs of his professors or the work and beliefs of Karl Barth. While it is true that both his professors and Barth influenced him, Bonhoeffer truly "found his way independently."

Near the beginning of *Sanctorum Communio*, Bonhoeffer sought to explain the Christian concept of personhood: "For Christian philosophy, the human person originates only in relation to the divine; the divine person transcends the human person, who both resists and is overwhelmed by the divine."[17] In other words, our personhood is rooted in the existence of God. Or as Stephen Nichols described Bonhoeffer's point, "Community with God and social community define personhood."[18] In this argumentation, Bonhoeffer harnessed a dichotomy he would use later in *Life Together*, namely the "I-Thou" relationship commonly associated with Martin Buber (1878–1965). Bonhoeffer argued that "for the individual to exist, 'others' must necessarily be there."[19] To be sure, Bonhoeffer was arguing for more than a trite "You complete me" perspective of God or other people. He wanted to affirm the importance of individuals deriving their personhood from God, but also how that same concept impacted relationships between individuals. Buber himself stated, "Through the *Thou* a man becomes *I*."[20] Bonhoeffer used the "I-Thou" relationship to describe how personhood, viewed from a Christian perspective, necessitates a social dynamic.[21] He argued, "Consequently, in some way the individual belongs essentially and absolutely with the other, according to God's will, even though, or precisely because, the one is completely separate from the other."[22] For Bonhoeffer, this was another way of stating, "It is not good that man should be alone" (Gen 2:18a).

The next two chapters of *Sanctorum Communio* dealt with sociological aspects of community and how sin breaks community. It is in the second of these two chapters that Bonhoeffer began to frame the foundational concept in *Sanctorum Communio* that runs through Bonhoeffer's entire career of thinking and writing about the church. All humanity in Adam, as Paul described in Romans 5, is interconnected underneath the headship of Adam. Bonhoeffer argued, "The structure of humanity-in-Adam is unique because it is both composed of many isolated individuals and yet is one, as the humanity that has sinned as a whole."[23] Bonhoeffer described this grouping of people underneath Adam as a collective person.[24] "It is 'Adam', a collective person, who can only be superseded by the collective person 'Christ existing as church-community.'"[25] Only Christ, the second Adam, and his community of followers replace the community of sinners following the first Adam. Every individual is a part of the collective person in Adam by virtue of their being born. Paul makes this very clear in his letter to the Romans: "Therefore, just as sin came into the world through one man, and death through sin, and so death spread to all men because all sinned" (Rom 5:12). Every Christian, through repentance and faith in Jesus, becomes a part of the collective person in Christ (see Rom 5:15–21). Through Bonhoeffer's development of the two notions of person (or individual) and collective person, Bonhoeffer described the relationship of Christ and the church, which is Christ existing as church-community. The church is Christ's collective person.

Bonhoeffer's development of these concepts displayed his brilliance. Such concepts also hinted at his oft-mentioned theological direction, namely that Christology was the theological center of the church. He was willing to enter into the context of the theological and philosophical thought of his time and repurpose it Christologically, even the work of someone like Hegel.

For Hegel, the way to think about the world was through dialectic or negation, pursuing truth by sifting through opposing sides of a particular topic.[26] Hegel argued for a radical, unbiblical understanding of the Godhead. He essentially denied the doctrine of the Trinity as the Bible reveals it.[27] However, Bonhoeffer did not share the unorthodox doctrine of God held by Hegel.[28] Bonhoeffer redeemed a phrase that Hegel had used to suit his argument and this phrase (Christ existing as church-community) stuck in Bonhoeffer's writing. This phrase, Christ existing as church-community, is another way of describing Christ as a collective person. Mark Devine rightly balances Bonhoeffer's intent in crafting this phrase: "The point was neither to reduce Christ's or God's presence to its manifestations among Christians in fellowship nor to confine divine activity within the church.

Rather, Bonhoeffer called for acknowledgment of the church as the sphere in which God is pleased to meet his children."[29] Other scholars have considered this phrase and the theological direction that followed to perhaps be Bonhoeffer's most important theological theme in all of his writing.[30] Bonhoeffer's doctrine of the church, first developed in *Sanctorum Communio* and closely tied to this theologically pregnant phrase, was decidedly focused on Christ.

These elements of Christ existing as church-community and Christ as a collective person found their way into *Life Together*. As Bonhoeffer was describing the place of the psalms in the Christian community's day together he said, "The Psalter is the vicarious prayer of Christ for his congregation. Now that Christ is with the Father, the new humanity in Christ—the body of Christ—on earth continues to pray his prayer to the end of time."[31] For Christ to pray the psalms for the Christian community requires a special kind of action on his part for the community. Jesus acted as what Bonhoeffer called a vicarious representative (someone who acts on behalf of another) or *Stellvertreter*.[32] In *Sanctorum Communio*, Bonhoeffer grounded his description of Christ as a vicarious representative in differentiating between Adam and Christ's headship: "In the old humanity the whole of humanity falls anew, so to speak, with every person who sins; in Christ, however, humanity has been brought once and for all—this is essential to *real* vicarious representative action—into community with God."[33] Christ worked to bring his people out of the collective person in Adam into his collective person. By grace through faith, Christians are brought out of being *in* Adam and are placed together *in* Christ.

It may be helpful to quickly recap these few rather thick concepts because they all intersect. Humanity's problem of sin places them in association with Adam in a collective person. Only Christ can redeem people from that fallen collective person in Adam. When Christ did that, he brought them into his collective person. This was Christ acting as a vicarious representative. He died in our place, for our sins. He took the punishment due our sins. He was the wrath-averting sacrifice that absorbed all the righteous judgment our sins rightly deserve. He continues to act as a vicarious representative for all those that have repented and believed in him. He intercedes for them, keeps them, and will return for them. In the meantime, the church is Christ's body; the church is Christ existing as church-community. He is living in, among, and through his body. That does not dissolve Christ away into an ethereal existence among the church. The King of kings is very much alive, living and reigning with the Father and the Holy Spirit, waiting for the day when he will come to consummate his kingdom. Christ existing as church-community means that Christ is living and reigning in and over his people in the world.

A wonderful detail about Bonhoeffer's writing of *Sanctorum Communio*, scholar Andrew Root has noted, is that he was teaching a children's Sunday school class at the same time: "As Bonhoeffer wrote about the concrete church, he was doing concrete ministry with children. Themes like *Stellvertretung* (place-sharing), objective spirit, and open/closed relationality may very well have had their creative origins, or at least gained energy, in his children's/youth ministry experience."[34] What a beautiful dichotomy! Bonhoeffer was wrestling with deep concepts and simultaneously trying to teach little children about the Bible. You may also notice in the quote from Root that instead of translating *Stellvertretung* or *Stellvertreter* as a vicarious representative action, he translated it as place-sharing (see 2 Cor 5:21), which he thought better captured the kind of advocate-like ministry that Jesus performed for his people.[35] Thus, place-sharing can be another way of describing Jesus's vicarious representative action for his people. Similarly, the apostle Paul declared, "For there is one God, and there is one mediator between God and men, the man Christ Jesus" (1 Tim 2:5). Whether one understands the terms Bonhoeffer used as vicarious representative action or place-sharing, he meant to also show that this work of Christ done on our behalf is meant to also propel us to mission. The Christian community must be filled with people grounded in the mediatorial work of Jesus who intercede for one another based on Christ's work. Such concepts are early elements of what would later materialize in *Life Together*.

THROUGH AND IN

Bonhoeffer asserted, "Christian community means community through Jesus Christ and in Jesus Christ."[36] Such a statement is one of the most concise yet powerful statements in *Life Together*. Bonhoeffer's emphasis on Christ and his relationship to the church is on full display in this sentence. The prepositions, *through* and *in*, exemplify the statement's main thrust. Christian community is emphatically Christocentric (Christ-centered), yet it is more than that: for the Christian community to be *through* Christ means that Jesus is not only the center but the creator of Christian community. Any community that is not *through* Christ is not Christian community. By being *in* Christ, the Christian community embodies the doctrine of the union with Christ. Put simply, believers are in union with Christ by grace through faith and thus in union with one another. Bonhoeffer's Lutheran framework inhibited him from using the specific phrase "union with Christ," as it is more common in the Reformed tradition. Yet, one scholar makes the case that Luther's view of the *communicatio idioma-tum* (the communication of attributes) between the two natures of Christ (human and divine) sets the path for Lutherans, like Bonhoeffer, to articulate what it means to be in union with Christ.[37] Elsewhere, it has been stated that a Lutheran take on union with Christ also has much to do with justification (being declared righteous by God): "Melanchthon held that believers were indwelled by Christ and therefore in union with him. But like Luther before him, he wanted to ensure that the ground for the believer's acceptance before the divine bar was found solely in Christ and his obedience."[38] Therefore, Bonhoeffer described Christian community as being grounded in union with Christ. The Lord Jesus is the creator of such community and the one by whom it is sustained.

Bonhoeffer also used the description of belonging to portray the relationship of one believer to another in Christian com-munity. As believers are individually in union with Christ, it follows that believers are collectively in union with Christ and one another. Thus, believers belong to Christ and to one another. Christians looking for belonging need look no further than the Christian community, because eternal belonging has been won for them in Jesus Christ. Such belonging is union with Christ and that union is shared by all Christians.[39]

THE THEME OF BELONGING
IN THE NEW TESTAMENT

The theme of belonging is pervasive in the New Testament. The apostle Paul's letters are thick with references to the unity of the church. "Likewise, my brothers, you also have died to the law through the body of Christ, so that you may belong to another, to him who has been raised from the dead, in order that we may bear fruit for God" (Rom 7:4). Through the death of Christ, Paul stated, Christians have died to the law and are no longer bound to it as they were before (Rom 7:1–3). They no longer belong to the law, but now to Christ. Though this is true individually for every believer, it is also true corporately for all believers: together we belong to Christ. Paul thus wrote to the church in Corinth: "and you are Christ's, and Christ is God's" (1 Cor 3:23). Paul pointed to a compounded belonging here: Christians belong to Christ, and Christ belongs to the Father.

Earlier in the same letter to Corinth, Paul discussed this corporate belonging: "To the church of God in Corinth, to those sanctified in Christ Jesus, called to be saints together with all those who in every place call upon the name of our Lord Jesus Christ, both their Lord and ours" (1 Cor 1:2). The church in Corinth, like every other church, was called to be saints together with all other believers in Christ. Paul had in view a corporate belonging to Christ of all believers. As Gordon Fee rightly put it, "In the new people that God is creating for himself in the coming age that has already dawned, the Corinthians have a share with all the saints, fellow believers "in every place" who also "call on the name of our Lord Jesus Christ," that is, who have put their trust in him and pray to and worship him."[40]

Christians have a share with fellow believers, because of their fellowship with Jesus. "God is faithful, by whom you were called into the fellowship of his Son, Jesus Christ our Lord" (1 Cor 1:9). "The calling *to* Christ is a calling to be *in fellowship with* Christ through the Spirit."[41] Christians' fellowship with Jesus is a spiritual one in which all believers share. "The Spirit himself bears witness with our spirit that we are children of God, and if children, then heirs—heirs of God and fellow heirs with Christ, provided that we suffer with him in order that we may also be glorified with him" (Rom 8:16–17). Paul made a similar statement to the church in Galatia:

For in Christ Jesus you are all sons of God, through faith.
For as many of you as were baptized into Christ have put
on Christ. There is neither Jew nor Greek, there is neither slave nor free, there is no male and female, for you
are all one in Christ Jesus. And if you are Christ's, then
you are Abraham's offspring, heirs according to promise.
(Gal 3:26-29)

In the words of Thomas Schreiner, "The inheritance becomes
a reality through union with Christ, the true seed of Abraham
(Gal. 3:16). Those who are united with Christ share in the inheritance that he has gained for them."[42] They are co-heirs of the
kingdom of God. This echoes Bonhoeffer's emphasis on Christian
community being *through* and *in* Christ. Biblically, this is visible
through the fellowship believers share with Christ and subsequently with one another.

The letter to the Ephesians is loaded with the language of
belonging. Paul argued that in revealing the gospel "which he
lavished upon us, in all wisdom and insight making known to
us the mystery of his will, according to his purpose, which he
set forth in Christ as a plan for the fullness of time, to unite all
things in him, things in heaven and things on earth" (Eph 1:8-
10). The "in Christ" in Ephesians 1:9 and 1:10 upholds the nature
of community Bonhoeffer portrays. Additionally, the headship
of Christ supports the notion of Christian community being
through Christ, namely that the community formed by Christ
is being brought under his headship.

Paul declared that Christ has saved believers "and raised
us up with him and seated us with him in the heavenly places
in Christ Jesus" (Eph 2:6). "Believers are made alive through a
dynamic union with Christ, which has enabled them to participate in the benefits of Christ's resurrection and exaltation."[43] As

Andrew Lincoln commented on this verse, "Believers are seen as included in Christ, so what God accomplished for Christ he accomplished for him as the representative, the head of a new humanity."[44] Lincoln's comments bring together the importance of union with Christ and the headship of Christ in this passage. Thus, it should make us think about Bonhoeffer's notion of collective person.

Paul also focuses on belonging as it relates to the life of the believer. "For me to live is Christ, and to die is gain" (Phil 1:21). Christian hope of eternal life informs Paul's statement that dying is gain for the Christian, but the affirmation that living is Christ is seemingly less emphasized by many Christians. Certainly, it at least displays that the Christian's life is bound up with the Lord Jesus. Paul expanded on this notion of the life of believers being bound up with Christ in other texts: "For you have died, and your life is hidden with Christ in God. When Christ who is your life appears, then you also will appear with him in glory" (Col 3:3-4). Similar to Paul's statement about death in Romans 7:4, something new happens to the life of believers once they have died with Christ. When Paul wrote this to the church in Colossae, he was reminding them that their lives, both individually and corporately, were caught up in Christ and they would together appear with Christ in glory. For the Christian, he or she has died with Christ by grace through faith in the gospel. Similarly, Paul spoke of Jesus "who died for us so that whether we are awake or asleep we might live with him" (1 Thess 5:10).

Both Peter and John also dealt with the theme of belonging. Peter declared,

> But you are a chosen race, a royal priesthood, a holy nation, a people for his own possession, that you may proclaim the excellencies of him who called you out of

darkness into his marvelous light. Once you were not a people, but now you are God's people; once you had not received mercy, but now you have received mercy (1 Pet 2:9–10).

At the heart of this text is the notion that Christians were once without all the blessings derived from being in Christ. This is clear throughout Paul's letters and is at the core of Bonhoeffer's argument that God has created the Christian community. John, like Paul, emphasized fellowship with Christ:

That which we have seen and heard we proclaim also to you, so that you too may have fellowship with us; and indeed our fellowship is with the Father and with his Son Jesus Christ. ... If we say we have fellowship with him while we walk in darkness, we lie and do not practice the truth. But if we walk in the light, as he is in the light, we have fellowship with one another, and the blood of Jesus his Son cleanses us from all sin. (1 John 1:3, 6–7)

John showed the link between fellowship with Christ and the fellowship of believers. Scholar I. Howard Marshall puts it well: "Persons who cut themselves off from fellowship with other Christians cannot have fellowship with God. But if they are prepared to live by God's light, they will come into fellowship with them and with God himself."[45] Having fellowship with Christians and with God is a standard of the Christian life.

The Gospels and Acts also have various passages that uphold the theme of belonging. "Behold, the virgin shall conceive and bear a son, and they shall call his name Immanuel" (which means, God with us)" (Matt 1:23). God being with his people is the essence of Christian community. Without Christ, there is no Christian community. "For where two or three or gathered in my name, there am I among them" (Matt 18:20). The context of this verse deals with church discipline to be sure, but God's presence with his people is made plain. God is committed to being with his people. As was described in 1 John and in Paul's writing, faith and obedience are the entry points to being in God's family, and Jesus affirmed this: "For whoever does the will of my Father in heaven is my brother and sister and mother" (Matt 12:50). Jesus embodies the promise of belonging for Christians.

Jesus prayed for believers "that they may all be one, just as you Father, are in me, and I in you, that they also may be in us, so that the world may believe that you have sent me. The glory that you have given me I have given to them, that they may be one even as we are one, I in them and you in me, that they may become perfectly one, so that the world may know that you sent me and loved them even as you loved me" (John 17:21-23). Union with Christ and with the Father was at the heart of what Jesus prayed for believers. Leon Morris stated that union with Christ has a purpose: "It looks for the disciples to be 'brought to complete unity.' They already had a unity of sorts. But this unity is not regarded as being sufficient. There is be a closer unity, a 'perfected' unity. As in verse 21, the unity of believers is to impress the world."[46] The Lord displays his commitment to this unity by displaying his power as the creator of Christian community. In the New Testament, the theme of belonging is on full display, a belonging created, purchased, and maintained by the Lord Jesus.

THREE IMPORTANT ELEMENTS
OF CHRISTIAN COMMUNITY

Having established the New Testament basis for belonging to Christ and his people, it will be helpful to further consider Bonhoeffer's claim of Christian community being *through* and *in* Jesus. He further explained his idea in three distinct ways.

First, Christian community rests on the assumption that believers act as the presence of Christ to one another; Christians need others around them. As in justification, Christians receive grace from outside themselves and that pattern continues in and through the expression of Christian community. In speaking truth to one another, Christians thereby minister the grace of Christ to one another.[47] Bonhoeffer's theological forebear, Martin Luther (1483–1546), taught that every Christian was a priest, meaning that each Christian was a part of the one body of Christ, and each had the ability to understand the Scriptures (see Rom 12:4–8; 1 Cor 12:12). This did not set aside the need for pastors and teachers of the Scriptures, but faith brought people into God's holy priesthood where they had direct access to God (see 1 Pet 2:9; Rev 5:10).[48] The priesthood of believers was an important aspect of Bonhoeffer's perspective on Christian community. Bonhoeffer would teach the importance of this concept to the church, "Everyone needs the other as priest. Everyone [is] dependent on the other! Through this the members of the church-community are closely bound to one another."[49] Bonhoeffer, in line with Luther, decided that because Christians are together in Christ and can understand the Scriptures by the Spirit, thus they have the responsibility of ministering to one another.

Secondly, recognizing a horizontal dimension to the mediating work of Christ, Bonhoeffer explained how Jesus enables peaceful community: "Among human beings there is strife. 'He is our peace" (Eph 2:14), says Paul of Jesus Christ. In him, broken and divided humanity has become one. Without Christ there is discord between God and humanity and between one human being and another."[50] In the contemporary church, there is a great need for peace. Racial strife has plagued us, political division is rampant, opinions abound, and the same polarization that we see in the world, we see in the church. But what treasures are available to the church in the mediatorial work of Christ to bring about peace amid such challenges! Regarding Jews and Gentiles in the church, Paul said: "For [Christ] is our peace, who has made us both one and has broken down in his flesh the dividing wall of hostility by abolishing the law of commandments expressed in ordinances, that he might create in himself one new man in place of the two, so making peace, and might reconcile us both to God in one body through the cross, thereby killing the hostility" (Eph 2:14–16). Everything that we need for peace is found in the Lord Jesus. He literally embodies peace between two separated factions: Jews and Gentiles. When we fix our eyes and hearts on Jesus and pursue his will together humbly, what peace is available to our churches! Furthermore, Bonhoeffer began *Life Together* by quoting Psalm 133:1: "Behold, how good and pleasant it is when brothers dwell in unity!" A Christian community is one thing, but a peaceful Christian community is more in line with what the Lord Jesus intends for it to be.

Thirdly, from eternity God decreed to elect and save the church through Jesus taking on flesh, uniting the church with Christ and the church with itself for eternity. Therefore, true Christian community can only, always be about Christ and what he has done.[51] Receiving salvation from the Lord (see Rom 5:17; Col 2:6) initiates not only our eternal unity as saints but the possibility for Christian unity here on earth. The gravity of such a thought staggers the mind. Yet, this is what God has done in Christ for all his people. As the hymn states, "how rich a treasure we possess in Jesus Christ our Lord!"[52] And how rich a treasure is our unity, together, through Christ alone:

> What persons are in themselves as Christians, in their inwardness and piety, cannot constitute the basis of our community, which is determined by what those persons

are in terms of Christ. Our community consists solely in what Christ has done to both of us. ... I have community with others and will continue to have it only through Jesus Christ.[53]

Bonhoeffer again returns to the staggering fact of what God has done in Jesus. This and this alone is the foundation of Christian community.

CONCLUSION

Bonhoeffer captured the biblical center of Christian community: Jesus. The Lord Jesus is not only the center of Christian community, but he also upholds it. This is true in a broad sense when one considers the vastness of the global church and the historic church, but it is also true in a specific sense to every faithful local church. Jesus as the center of Christian community must not only be a theological emphasis in our beliefs, but it must be lived, preached, believed, prayed for, encouraged, and celebrated. Christ alone must be held up as the means for the existence and sustainment of Christian community.

CHAPTER 4

Community as Divine Reality

" I have eaten two enormous meals with a healthy appetite; in a word, I'm enjoying the ship as long as it can be enjoyed."[1] As Bonhoeffer set out on a journey to the United States on September 6, 1930, the twenty-four-year-old student wrote about his time on the ship to one of his regular correspondents— his grandmother. A busy summer had materialized into what would become an important trip for Bonhoeffer. Earlier in the summer of that year, Bonhoeffer completed his second church examination, which was part of his journey to ordination for the pastorate. Also, that summer he had the opportunity to eulogize one of his former mentors, Adolf von Harnack, who had unexpectedly died.[2] By September he ended his time as a voluntary assistant lecturer at the university in Berlin and set sail for the United States for a yearlong study grant at Union Seminary in New York.[3] His year in the United States would act as a sort of calm before the storm.

IN THE UNITED STATES

Before Bonhoeffer began his time under the Sloan Fellowship at Union Seminary, he spent five days visiting with relatives on his mother's side in Philadelphia. His aunt and uncle met him at the New York City harbor after his nine days at sea. They treated him to trips around the city of Philadelphia and lots of stories about their transition to life in the United States.[4] When this visit had come to an end and it was time to begin at Union, he found himself in the company of the two other Sloan Fellows with whom he became good friends: Erwin Sutz (1906–87), who was from Switzerland, and Jean Lassere (1908–83), who was from France. They became Bonhoeffer's European connection while in the United States.[5] Sutz was a student of Karl Barth and shared many theological commonalities with Bonhoeffer.[6] Lassere was the first pacifist minister that Bonhoeffer had ever met.[7] He remained in contact with both men after this time in the United States, and they left lasting theological impressions on him.

Bonhoeffer also made other important friends while in America. Frank Fisher (1908–60) was a fellow student at Union and an African American. Bonhoeffer was deeply interested in the African American community, and Fisher was his entrance into that world. Their friendship became substantial enough that Bonhoeffer spent much of his extra time on Sundays and throughout the week at the Abyssinian Baptist Church in Harlem. He not only worshipped there but also taught a Sunday school class and helped in the youth ministry.[8] Bonhoeffer loved the fervor of the African American services, and he rightly saw the burdens of racism and injustice under which these brothers and sisters lived and worshipped.[9] Bonhoeffer's friendship with Fisher provided him with transformative experiences that would soon provide practical lessons to apply in his own country. Bonhoeffer wrote about his experience in the Harlem church upon his return to Berlin: "Here one really could still hear someone talk in a Christian sense about sin and grace and the love of God and ultimate hope, albeit in a form different from that to which we are accustomed. In contrast to the often lecturelike character of the "white" sermon, the "black Christ" is preached with captivating passion and vividness."[10] It appears Bonhoeffer's time in Harlem was unique from anything he experienced at Union and had a transformative impact on his view of ministry and the church.

Bonhoeffer's other American friend was Paul Lehmann (1906–94), who grew closer to him than any other classmate at Union. Lehmann had hoped for years after their first meeting, that Bonhoeffer would come back to the United States to become a professor.[11] But Bonhoeffer never felt called to make such a move.

Bonhoeffer was not impressed by what he experienced in the theological climate in America. He bemoaned the sentimentality among the intellectuals in the theological liberalism at Union. He was disappointed by the immaturity displayed in class discussions and the unwillingness to take study seriously. Bonhoeffer was intrigued by Reinhold Niebuhr (1892–1971), one of the professors he studied with at Union. However, Bonhoeffer was willing to openly challenge Niebuhr's views, which were shaped by the Social Gospel movement. The Social Gospel movement was primarily an American phenomenon wherein liberal Protestants sought to find biblically informed ways to deal with societal issues. The movement was generally marked by a belief that the kingdom of God needed to be brought into the present by addressing societal issues and injustices. Among those in the history of the movement, there was a prevailing thought that Christians could help bring the kingdom to earth and thus, they could display a kind of utopian perspective. Detractors would accuse the Social Gospel movement of diluting or setting aside the gospel message itself.[12] Reinhold Niebuhr advocated a type of Christian realism, which consistently tried to steer away from any type of transcendence in the Christian life. Bonhoeffer saw Niebuhr as lacking confessional vitality.[13] He saw the same pervasive problems not just at Union: "In New York, they preach about virtually everything; only one thing is not addressed, or addressed so rarely that I have as yet been unable to hear it, namely, the gospel of Jesus Christ, the cross, sin and forgiveness, death and life."[14] Needless to say, he was ready to make his way back home to Berlin once his time at Union was complete. He managed to fit in a trip to Cuba in the middle of his time in America around Christmas with Erwin Sutz.[15] He also went on a long trip at the end of the academic year with Sutz, Lassere, and Lehmann.[16] In 1931, he finally made his way back to Germany in the middle of the year to begin a new chapter in his life.

NEW CAREERS

This new chapter would be quite busy for Bonhoeffer. He was not home long from the United States when he began traveling again. This time, he was on his way to Bonn, Switzerland to have his first visit with Karl Barth. Erwin Sutz had arranged the meeting while Bonhoeffer was still in the United States.[17] This meeting began a relationship that continued until Bonhoeffer's death. Finally, Bonhoeffer was able to meet the man who had had such an impact on him through his writing. Writing to his parents later about the meeting, he said, "I have now met Barth and got to know him quite well at a discussion evening at his house. I like him very much indeed and am also very impressed by his lectures."[18] His visit with Barth did not last long and soon he was back in Berlin to begin three new careers.

Bonhoeffer took on the role of an assistant lecturer at the University of Berlin, which paid a meager salary.[19] He also began official ecumenical work having received an invitation to the World Alliance for Promoting International Friendship Through the Churches.[20] His third career was as a chaplain to students at the Berlin Technical University.[21] Bethge summed up this busy time for Bonhoeffer well: "He now began to teach on a faculty whose theology he did not share, and to preach in a church whose self-confidence he regarded as unfounded. More aware than before, he now became part of a society that was moving toward political, social, and economic chaos."[22] The preaching he did was during his work as a chaplain but after his official ordination to the ministry in November 1931.[23]

In February 1932, Bonhoeffer moved out of his family's home to another part of town, northeast Berlin, which put him in another district of service in the church. When his chaplaincy was over around the same time, he requested the post of pastoral assistant at a church around the corner from his house.[24] He described this part of town in a letter to Erwin Sutz: "[It] is about the toughest neighborhood of Berlin, with the most difficult socioeconomic and political conditions."[25] This was right where Bonhoeffer wanted to be, despite its differences from the type of area he was used to residing in with his parents. His charge was among the youth of the congregation, specifically getting young, rowdy boys to their confirmation. He also regularly met with the families of his confirmands. He grew close to those under his pastoral care, inviting them to his house for Bible study and to listen to records of African American spirituals he brought home from the United States.[26]

It was in this period, on which he would later reflect, that he felt that he came to the Bible and was converted.[27] Amid the demanding schedule of three careers and the burdens of ministry, Bonhoeffer came to know the Lord Jesus through the Scriptures. Some family and friends who knew him well during this time grew concerned and suspicious of the changes in his life; his newfound devotion and religious fervor were that noticeable.[28] So many experiences in the providence of the Lord were coming together in the wonderful, messy mosaic of Bonhoeffer's life.

DEVELOPMENTS IN "THE NATURE OF THE CHURCH" LECTURES

The summer of 1932 found Bonhoeffer lecturing at the University of Berlin. The course that he taught was titled "The Nature of the Church." Bethge gave insight into Bonhoeffer's approach to the class and how it was received by the students:

> Having established his theological standpoint, Bonhoeffer presented his first attempt at a lecture using the topic of his own starting point: the church. He announced two-hour lectures and, despite being a passionate late-sleeper, forced himself to begin teaching at eight o'clock in the morning. The lecture hall began to fill; people had expectations of both critique and concreteness.[29]

It was an opportunity for him to lecture on many of the themes he had developed in *Sanctorum Communio*. These lectures were broken down into two main parts: The Place of the Church and The Form of the Church. The second part was predominantly an opportunity to wrestle with the concepts of Christ existing as church-community, Christ as a collective person, and Christ's vicarious representative action.[30]

He began by defining the church by looking at its form: "The church as a genuine form is unity, basically the unity of God! The form reveals itself under the presupposition of unity. ... The church is primary unity. Those who do not start with unity confuse the church with a religious community."[31] Bonhoeffer's declaration of the church as unity shows his emphasis on the body of Christ having existed from eternity. Knowing Bonhoeffer's emphasis on Christ as a collective person, one can see how he described the form of the church to be Christ-shaped. With an eye toward justification, Bonhoeffer declared, "One stands for all; Christ is the vicarious representative of humanity. Adam [stands] not in [the] place of the other but rather in his own. Christ stands [in] place of humanity!"[32] Bonhoeffer connected justification to Christ's vicarious representative action by walking through four vital elements of Christ's completion of his task: his incarnation, his active obedience, his death on the cross, and his resurrection.[33] What stands out from his lectures is that while his subject was the church, he spent a significant amount of time talking about Christ.

Bonhoeffer also explained the participation of the Holy Spirit in the formation of the church: "The Holy Spirit actualized that which has been realized through Christ."[34] Bonhoeffer was biblically faithful in this distinction showing that the Holy Spirit is he who binds the church together in Christ (Rom 8:9–11).[35] Such an orthodox view kept the church from being viewed as anything less than what God made it to be. "Church [is not to be understood] as a religious community! Church is [a] reality of faith. [An] ideal of experience, rather than [of] reality, [that] is religious community."[36] Bonhoeffer had clearly taken his initial assertions in *Sanctorum Communio* and not only stayed faithful to them but expanded on and applied them.

REFINEMENTS IN THE
CHRISTOLOGY LECTURES

One year later in the summer semester of 1933, Bonhoeffer taught a course on Christology, the study of Christ. He believed that, "Only scholarship that knows itself to be within the realm of the Christian church could agree here that Christology is the center of the realm of scholarship itself."[37] For those who would take Bonhoeffer's Christocentrism as detrimental to a proper confession of the Trinity, Dane Ortlund provides helpful counsel: "Christocentrism can happily co-exist with orthodox trinitarianism because (1) it is only through Christ that we know of the Trinity, and (2) the Trinity itself is Christ-centered. As we view the Trinity through Christ and Christ through the Trinity, we find orthodox trinitarianism and Christocentrism not only compatible but mutually reinforcing."[38] Therefore, Bonhoeffer's approach to Christology as being central to theology is not a cause for concern. Christology was the lens through which he described the church, by showing that Christ is central to understanding it.

A development of Bonhoeffer's propositions of Christ existing as church-community or as collective person was expanded in these lectures. He stated, "The being of Christ's person is essentially relatedness to me. His being-Christ is his being-for-me. This pro-me is not to be understood as an effect that issues from Christ or as a form that he assumes incidentally but is to be understood as the being of his very person. The very core of his person is pro-me."[39] In other words, this meant that Christ is "for" his people. Such a position was not a great leap for Bonhoeffer to make, especially since he had established the concept of Christ's vicarious representative action for Christians.[40] Therefore, Christ is *for* his church.

One additional element that came out of Bonhoeffer's Christology lectures not previously stated in *Sanctorum Communio* or his lectures on the church had to do with how Christ exists as church-community. As he explained this theme's connection to the sacrament of communion, Bonhoeffer stated, "The concept of the body as applied to the church-community is not a functional concept referring to members but is instead a concept of the way in which the Christ exists who is present, exalted, and humiliated."[41] Bonhoeffer's words show the importance of keeping the cross integral to the church's ongoing understanding of Christology. The words of H. Gaylon Barker help grasp Bonhoeffer's point: "Christ *pro me*, the humiliated and risen Christ existing as church-community, is the center of human existence. Standing between God and humanity, in fact, standing in humanity's place before God, Christ stands at the center of the new humanity, at the center of human existence and history."[42] Bonhoeffer provocatively picked up this point later in his lectures: "History finds its meaning in the humiliation of Christ."[43] Because Christians are rooted in Christ, Christian suffering is not meaningless, because the Lord of the church suffered on her behalf. Christ's sufferings for his people give meaning to the suffering his people endure as they follow him. These rich Christological developments led to that which was later lived and taught at his underground seminary in Finkenwalde.

CHRISTIAN COMMUNITY A DIVINE REALITY

In *Life Together*, Bonhoeffer vehemently stated that Christian community cannot be anything other than what Jesus has intended it to be. From this statement, two central things must be affirmed. First, "Christian community is not an ideal, but a divine reality."[44] Second, "Christian community is a spiritual and not a psychic reality."[45] The first of these two ideas will be considered in this chapter and the second will be considered in the next.

In explaining the first important point about Christian communities, Bonhoeffer used the terms "wishful image,"[46] "dream,"[47] and "wishful dream"[48] to describe the ways Christian community is often viewed apart from Christ. This can happen anytime a Christian community is structured around personal preferences, rather than how Christ calls Christian community to be. Such dreams born from inclinations of members or leaders can be the cause for destruction of true Christian community. Community built on dreams is not built on the gospel and therefore does not rest on gospel promises. True Christian community is received from God as a gift.[49] Bonhoeffer explained, "Like the Christian's sanctification, Christian community is a gift of God to which we have no claim. Only God knows the real condition of either our community or our sanctification."[50]

Maybe you have experienced this. A Bible study group, a small group, or even a church of which you are a part suddenly starts to look more like a member's preference rather than how the Scriptures would have it look. The Bible is not central anymore because the intention is just to do life together. The group molds around a specific schedule because that is what a certain person prefers. The person who speaks the loudest generally dictates what the group does or studies. The church does not really want older people or younger people to come because it would mess up the culture of the congregation. Such things are examples of the kinds of things that can happen when human ideals rule in communities.

How seemingly *right* it feels to clamor about how a community should be. That is not to say that Christian community should not have a goal that all involved share. However, one must grapple with the pervasive issue that the members of Christian community have opinions of how the community should be. Some would argue that their preferences are grounded in the demands of Scripture, while others, if they are honest, are operating under their own preferences. The concept of an ideal Christian community was not necessarily something that Bonhoeffer was against. The question was *whose* ideal? The answer was clear for Bonhoeffer—God determines what the *ideal* Christian community should be. This is partly what Bonhoeffer meant when he said, "Christian community is not an ideal, but a divine reality."[51] The divine *ideal* is a reality. God's ideal or God's vision for a Christian community (or church), is what matters.

Bonhoeffer's insistence that Christian community is already a divine reality also displays a combination of theological and practical thinking regarding community. Part of the genius Bonhoeffer displayed in *Life Together* is the ability to oscillate between theological foundations and practical applications. This statement is an excellent example. The second half of the statement builds off the earlier argument that Christian community is through Christ or namely that Jesus is its creator. For community to be a divine reality implies that it is not a human product or creation. It is created by God before humans have anything to do with it. This is in line with God's salvific work in which he gives his love and grace. Salvation, as well as God's love and grace, are all divine realities before they are human realities. Though people may desire community and even consider it an ideal to be striven for, Christian community is not born out of human desire or ideal but is given in the divine reality. This has all kinds of practical implications for a Christian community, but the greatest is to refrain from making desires and ideals for community the driving force of the community. Bonhoeffer emphatically stated, "Because God has already laid the only foundation of our community, because God has united us in one body with other Christians in Jesus Christ long before we entered into common life with them, we enter into that life together with other Christians, not as those who make demands, but as those who thankfully receive."[52] Since Christian community, like salvation, belongs to the Lord and he is its creator, Christians receive and participate in this community.

What about all of the well-intentioned vision casting that takes place in our churches today? Leaders pore over the Scriptures and seek the Lord in prayer, attempting to discern God's will for their congregations. Many churches wrestle with how they should handle growth: build a bigger building, have more services, or multiply the church through church planting. Others think about creative ways to reach out to their communities with the gospel. Has Bonhoeffer demonized this work of vision casting? The answer is: *maybe*. Bonhoeffer said, "Every human idealized image that is brought into the Christian community is a hindrance to genuine community and must be broken up so that genuine community can survive."[53] Part of the work in which leaders take part in defining vision must be to sift out human idealized images. So perhaps one of the solutions of dealing with church growth is just a preference and not actually a godly or wise course of action. Maybe the new outreach idea is just that, an idea, and it needs more prayer and careful thought. On a grand scale, Bonhoeffer saw the result of Christian community being made in the image of man in the society in which he lived. Much of the church in Germany had given in to the Nazi impulses. The rampant racism and anti-Semitism of the Nazi party had sadly gone unchallenged by many. The Nazi flag and other symbols were displayed over church altars, giving the depiction that God approved of Nazi agendas. Yet, one need not have Nazis in the church for it to be in danger of being made in the image of man. Bonhoeffer declared, "Those who love their dream of a Christian community more than the Christian community itself become destroyers of that Christian community even though their personal intentions may be ever so honest, earnest, and sacrificial."[54] The more a Christian community is made in the image of a human ideal, the less room it has to develop God's intended reality for his bride.

Thus, seeking the Lord for a *vision* for one's Christian community is not entirely problematic. The challenge comes, as Bonhoeffer would likely affirm when the divine reality begins to challenge one's ideal. Is the leader willing to admit when his ideal is not in line with the divine reality? Meaning, are we willing to lay down our ideals when they do not align with God's standard he has shown us in the Scriptures?

Moses was not given the freedom to make the tabernacle according to his ideal, but according to the reality that God showed him. "Exactly as I show you concerning the pattern of the tabernacle, and of all its furniture, so you shall make it" (Exod 25:9). Why would the community of the risen Lord Jesus Christ be any different? The author to the Hebrews takes this further, pointing to the divine reality of the heavenly things associated with Jesus's atoning work: "the greater and more perfect tent" into which Christ entered (Heb 9:11–12), "the heavenly things" of which the earthly were but a copy were purified with the blood of Christ (Heb 9:23), Christ entered heaven itself to make atonement for us (Heb 9:24), and the law calls for sacrifices that are but shadows of "the true form of these realities" (Heb 10:1). Therefore, more important than Bonhoeffer's distinctions, Scripture itself points to the theme of a heavenly reality. So much of the Christian life consists of living in light of heavenly realities. God has been clear that churches are to be focused on the person and work of Jesus. God has been clear that the ministry of the Word and prayer ought to be central to the ministry offered by our churches. God has been clear about the character and abilities needed by elders and deacons who lead in our churches. God has been clear about the gospel of Jesus, which makes God's enemies into his sons and daughters. The clarity we have received from God in the Scriptures ought to lead us toward God's vision for our churches.

RECEIVED NOT MADE

The very foundation of the gospel message is predicated on reception: "For I delivered to you as of first importance what I also received: that Christ died for our sins in accordance with the Scriptures" (1 Cor 15:3). So too, the commands for how the Lord is to be worshipped by the church are received: "For I received from the Lord what I also delivered to you, that the Lord Jesus on the night when he was betrayed took bread" (1 Cor 11:23). It also follows that Jesus's position of lordship over one's body and soul has to be received by faith (Rom 3:25, 5:17; 1 Cor 4:7; Col 2:6). In terms of how a Christian relates to God, one might say it is better to receive. All that a believer has in Christ has been received. Nothing good was brought to the relationship by the believer. Therefore, the way that Christians interact with Christian community is by receiving it, not by making it. This does not mean that Christians do not work as a Christian community is formed, it simply means that Christians do not stand as creators over the community to be its lord. That position is taken by the Lord Jesus. Bonhoeffer said, "The more thankfully we daily receive what is given to us, the more assuredly and consistently will community increase and grow from day to day as God pleases."[55] Thus, Christian community ought to be daily received thankfully and God will give the increase.

The potential danger in that idea is for a lovely, abstract concept to end up having little to do with real life. In other words, how does one *receive* Christian community? Lovely-sounding, tweetable thoughts are just that unless they can be lived. The answer for how Christian community is to be received is inherent in Bonhoeffer's assertion that Christian community is a divine reality. Since all of the Christian life is fed from the well of divine reality, it stands to follow that Christian community flows from that same well. In other words, when a person is saved by grace through faith in the Lord Jesus, they are in right relationship with God, and also automatically become part of the community in his Son. Thus, while the Christian life is an exercise in living out individually who we are in Jesus Christ, so the same is true corporately. So, the onus is on a congregation to live out together who they are in Christ. Because Christian community is born out of the gospel message, it may be helpful to consider how the gospel is to be received to know how Christian community is to be received.

Receiving the gospel requires humility. Jesus said, "Truly, I say to you, whoever does not receive the kingdom of God like a child shall not enter it" (Mark 10:15). Jesus's statement in this verse is one of the most oft-repeated verses in the Bible, but also has the potential of being misunderstood. Sometimes, this verse can be understood as though Jesus is recommending a never-ending childish outlook on Jesus and faith. In other words, Jesus was advocating to never grow up. Rather, when Jesus talks about being "like a child," he is encouraging a humble, joyful, and trusting reception of the kingdom (see also Acts 17:11; Heb 12:28; Jas 1:21).

Receiving the gospel adds such childlike people to the family of God. "He came to his own, and his own people did not receive him. But to all who did receive him, who believed in his name, he gave the right to become children of God, who were born, not of blood nor of the will of the flesh nor of the will of man, but of God" (John 1:11–13). Many who were Jesus's own people—his fellow Jews—did not receive him. A common response to Jesus is rejection and not reception. However, those who have received him through faith in his name have become part of the family of God.

Receiving the gospel message involves repentance and faith. The apostle Peter's sermon on the day of Pentecost reflected this as he called his listeners to repent and believe. Those who responded were then baptized, being brought into the church (Acts 2:38–41). Paul often reiterated the need to respond to or receive the word by faith (see Rom 3:25; Gal 3:2). This "hearing with faith" required an ongoing life of repentance wherein sin was to be put to death in the lives of those who have responded by faith (see Rom 8:13; Heb 10:26).

Reception of the gospel message produces action. Paul warned the Corinthians of the possibility of their having received the grace of God in vain (2 Cor 6:1). The message of the gospel communicated by the grace of God is not meant to fall flat upon those that hear, instead, God's grace changes its recipients. "Therefore, as you received Christ Jesus the Lord, so walk in him" (Col 2:6). Such obedience is expected of those who have received the gospel message. This grace-empowered obedience then serves as an example to other believers to do the same. (see Phil 4:9; 1 Thess 1:6). Obedience-producing reception also pleases God (1 Thess 4:1).

Each of these biblical examples of receiving the gospel has immediate importance for the Christian community. Such themes (humility, the theme of the family of God, repentance and faith, and obedience) must be part of the Christian community, but also how one receives the Christian community. Salvation brings us into relationship with God, but it also brings us into relationship with God's family. The two cannot be separated. Bonhoeffer stated, "Christian community is not an ideal we have to realize, but rather a reality created by God in Christ in which we may participate. The more clearly we learn to recognize that the ground and strength and promise of all our community is in Jesus Christ alone, the more calmly we will learn to think about our community and pray and hope for it."[56] Bonhoeffer is stating that, for God, Christian community is, just as every Christian's salvation is. As David says, "Such knowledge is too wonderful for me; it is high; I cannot attain it" (Ps 139:6). No greater foundation exists for Christian community than that God spoke it into being.

Practically speaking, Bonhoeffer cautions the church from thinking that she creates Christian community in the same way people would create a sewing group. Believers in Christ *get to* participate in the glorious fellowship they have together with the risen Lord Jesus. They receive this great blessing in the same way they received salvation. Such ongoing reception is how the Lord gives this gift of Christian community to his people. In this, God receives all the glory.

CONCLUSION

In Christian community, we receive from God his intended design for our lives as Christians. That design has a corporate shape to it. When we begin from the context of the gospel message setting us free from sin and incorporating us into a body, we guard ourselves from making community about our preferences and opinions. We continue to look to God's design as is revealed in the Scriptures in order to know how our individual Christian lives should be ordered as well as our corporate Christian lives. Relying on God's will displayed in the Word protects us from ourselves and helps our Christian communities to adorn the gospel.

CHAPTER 5

Community as Spiritual

" **T**o the fellow student who has now felt compelled to remove this notice for the third time! Dear Friend: Why so secretive and why always the same joke, or why so terribly angry? ... Why not come round to see me sometime?"[1] In the spirit of Luther, Bonhoeffer posted a notice at the Technical College at which he was serving as a chaplain in late 1932. It appears a student kept removing the schedule of chaplain activities and Bonhoeffer was not intending to back down. He was prepared to take up the challenge. Furthermore, he posted this note along with the schedule of activities for a fourth time on letterhead with his personal address.[2] As the chaplain for the school, Bonhoeffer knew that his effective ministry to the students required him to get his hands dirty. However, two-thirds of the students he was to serve were members of the Nazi student group.[3] Bonhoeffer had his hands full; nevertheless, he saw his task as an important gospel ministry even in such an environment.

Bonhoeffer's challenging experiences in this season of his life display an important aspect of Christian community—it is hard. Something must guide the community and protect it from becoming something other than what God would have it to be.

The practical way that a Christian community is maintained by God is through the ministry of the Holy Spirit. That can be confusing for some, meaning how do we know when the Holy Spirit is leading? The Holy Spirit always seeks to teach about Jesus and remind believers about the truth about Jesus in the revealed Word (John 14:26; 15:26). Therefore, when the Spirit is leading, he is producing Christ-honoring fruit in individuals and in the community. We see this core concept of the Holy Spirit in relation to Christian community both through some of the aspects of Bonhoeffer's life, but also through his writing on the topic in *Life Together*.

CHANGES FOR BONHOEFFER AND 1933

Several shifts began to happen in Bonhoeffer as 1933 began. The first was theological. He began to move away from the technicalities embodied in his dissertation and postdoctoral thesis and toward theology developed from his own words. This season started to lay the foundation for what would become *Cost of Discipleship* and *Life Together*. The second shift he experienced focused on his faith and his view of the Bible.[4] Years after this time, this transformation was best described in the letter Bonhoeffer wrote to his friend Elisabeth Zinn (1908–95) describing his conversion.[5]

Bonhoeffer had been transformed and it was apparent in his ministry work as well as in his writing. In the winter semester that began at the end of 1932, Bonhoeffer gave a series of lectures on the first three chapters of the book of Genesis, which would later be published as *Creation and Fall*. Bonhoeffer considered the work a theological exposition of the Genesis account of creation and the fall of mankind. This was coincidentally the first book by Bonhoeffer that Barth would read.[6] It has been noted that this book was Bonhoeffer's attempt to let the Bible speak to and against the environment brewing around him.[7] German societal stability began to unravel in 1933 and Bonhoeffer was in the middle of it all.

The year 1933 became a redirecting force in his life and ministry. Not only did Bonhoeffer's life change, but Germany and all of the world changed. Bonhoeffer could not have escaped it. When Adolf Hitler (1889–1945) took over the leadership of the government in January 1933, it changed everything.[8] As Germany was swept up into the mesmerizing power of the *Führer*, many of the churches and seminary faculties were influenced by the rhetoric as well. The notion of the *Führer* principle dictated that political authority in the government came from the top down through all lower levels of life. The top, from which all authority flowed, was the *Führer*. This changed not only political life but every aspect of German society and with it, the churches.[9]

In February, Bonhoeffer was invited to give an address on the radio. It was entitled "The Younger Generation's Altered View of the Concept of *Führer*." During the live broadcast, while he was reading through his transcript, someone at the radio station switched off his microphone, and the rest of his address was not heard on the radio. He had the transcript printed and circulated afterward.[10] He also later gave the address at the Technical University and the College of Political Science.[11] Bonhoeffer saw the dangers of what was taking place and he was no longer able to be politically passive. From this time on, Bonhoeffer referred to Hitler as the Antichrist.[12] In March, the Enabling Act was passed, which gave Hitler and his cabinet the power to enact laws without the involvement of the Reichstag (the parliament). This step, along with the Malicious Practices Acts passed after the Reichstag fire in late February, brought about total Nazi control. The same week the Enabling Act was passed, the first concentration camp in Dachau was opened.[13] Evil was spreading throughout Germany.

Soon after he assumed the role of Chancellor, Hitler began his campaign of *Gleichschaltung* (literally, "switching into the same gear") of German society."[14] Hitler was essentially fighting for the same kind of devotion and passion for the nation and its imminent thousand-year Third Reich as Christians would have for their faith in Christ.[15] A year before this, the German Christian movement began in May 1932.[16] The German Christians absorbed some of the rhetoric inherent in Hitler's vision for a mighty German Reich.[17] Given Germany's historic blend of nationalism and Christian faith, it is not hard to fathom such a group as the German Christians existing. Larry Rasmussen pointed out,

> In the very early months of National Socialism, the party even encouraged Germans to rejoin the church (they did), and Hitler seemed to offer a pseudo-religious and populist, even mystical, transformation of politics itself. Clergy and laity in turn reciprocated with enthusiasm for what they regarded as the opportunity to re-evangelize the nation and rejuvenate the church.[18]

The tainting of Christianity with populist political agendas was the mire from which the German Christian movement arose. Their stance on confessional issues and their very existence sparked much of the resulting opposition that arose in the church thereafter.

In April, the Aryan paragraph was passed by the Reichstag, which removed all Jews from civil service, which included churches, both Catholic and Protestant. The majority church in Germany was largely complicit in the order, which gave Hitler the ability to establish one unified Reich Church. To keep his will maintained in the churches, Hitler appointed a special representative to the churches. Hitler's special representative was made Reich Bishop by July, winning more than 70 percent of the vote. Also voted in and approved that July by the Reich Church was the Aryan paragraph.[19]

Bonhoeffer was driven to action. He wrote an essay titled "The Church and the Jewish Question," which was published in a Protestant magazine for culture and politics. One of Bonhoeffer's biographers commented on the apparent struggle Bonhoeffer had going against the Lutheran Church's understanding that the state had the responsibility to uphold law and order in the world. In some ways, the church had no context for how to speak theologically against the state. However, as the same biographer pointed out, in this essay Bonhoeffer was beginning to formulate a way forward. The state had encroached on the church with the Aryan paragraph, thus the church needed to know how to respond.[20]

With the implementation of the Reich Church and Hitler's man as Reich Bishop, the struggle for the church in Germany was underway. A movement called the Young Reformation Movement for the Renewal of the Church sprang up as an attempt to correct what was happening at the hands of the Nazi government. However, the Young Reformation movement was not so much against the Nazi government but rather against the state's encroachment into the church. The German Christian movement was allowing the state to interfere, and the Young Reformation sought to correct that. The result of their efforts was the start of the German Evangelical Church. The creation of this new church failed as Hitler's man became Reich Bishop and the German Evangelical Church fell under his control.[21]

THE ROAD TO BETHEL

Bonhoeffer spoke at a Young Reformation meeting in June pushing hard against the Aryan paragraph and what the church must do in response. He did not receive a great hearing from those in attendance. However, a few there appreciated Bonhoeffer's zeal and vision for the future of the church concerning these issues.[22] The failure of the German Evangelical Church solidified in the elections in July brought about a new direction for those that thought like Bonhoeffer. In August, groups of pastors gathered in Westphalia at a hospital called Bethel to begin drafting what would be called the Bethel Confession. This statement was intended to push against the false doctrine of the German Christians. Though Bonhoeffer was involved with the Bethel Confession, he was not happy with its lack of confessional strength.

In September 1933, the church in the Old Prussian Union held its synod and it was overrun by the German Christians. It was referred to as the brown synod because so many showed up wearing brown SA military uniforms.[23] A notable result of the synod was a vote to only allow Nazi party members and sympathizers as well as those who were only of Aryan descent to be allowed to serve in the church. Thus, the church had voted to enact the Aryan Paragraph. This led to the creation of the Pastors' Emergency League, which replaced the Young Reformation movement. The League grew quickly to nearly six thousand pastors.[24] The League was founded by Martin Niemöller (1892-1984), who served as pastor of the Dahlem church in Berlin. Niemöller arose as the primary leader of the opposition against the German Christian movement.[25]

Toward the end of September 1933, Niemöller sent a flyer on behalf of the Pastor's Emergency League to the National Synod, which represented the German Evangelical Church. The flyer stated in part, "The National Synod must not give the impression, through its solemn character, that it represents a united church, as long as our congregations are torn apart by the deepest conflicts."[26] The flyer pointed to the existence of dissenting voices among the German Evangelical Church, though it was supposed to be a cohesive body. As with most everything the Nazi government did, the German Evangelical Church was less an attempt at actual unity and simply a well-dressed ploy of *Gleichschaltung*. Bonhoeffer was among those who drafted the statement printed on the flyer and his name is listed among the rest of the pastors involved.[27] The dissenting voices in the brewing church struggle were multiplying. The Confessing Church was thus born, having its governing council democratically elected in October, which was a first among German Protestant Churches.[28] Nevertheless, the Confessing Church was not perfect.

Nazi influence was felt even within the reform movement. Bonhoeffer worked to keep the Aryan paragraph and the general beliefs of the Nazi party even out of the Confessing Church. For such efforts, he met formidable criticism. After all, every other political party besides the Nazi party was considered illegal on June 14.[29] A professor at the University of Göttingen, Paul Althaus (1888-1966), had joined the ranks of dissenting pastors only to eventually begin singing the praises of the Nazi movement from within the Confessing Church. Subsequently, the final version of the Bethel Confession would have any criticism of the Aryan paragraph removed. Bonhoeffer was devastated.[30] Before the final version was drafted, Bonhoeffer decided to take leave of the situation and accept a pastorate. The events of this year are what moved him to London. Bonhoeffer's friend Bethge wrote, "Thus Bonhoeffer left Berlin partly because of doubts about the course he should take and partly to keep his thoughts and actions from being constricted into a narrow ecclesiastical dimension. What he wanted was a period of seeking and testing in a small, quiet congregation."[31] Bonhoeffer wrote to Friedrich Singer (1873-1934), the pastor he would be replacing in London, that he would be arriving on October 17.[32] Thus he began a nearly two-year period of physical disconnect from the church struggle in Germany.

Bonhoeffer took up his pastorate in London in October, and his work on the confession continued.[33] His distance from Berlin and the political infiltration that had been taking place resulted in the confession losing its original potency.[34] Bonhoeffer outlined the specific problems he saw in the final version of the Bethel Confession in a talk he gave at a pastors' conference in Bradford, Yorkshire, England in November 1933. The primary issues were with key theological points like justification, the cross, and the Holy Spirit.[35] Bonhoeffer felt that a key leader had acted to dilute the confession and keep it from having the kind of impact it could or should have had.[36] The notes from Bonhoeffer's comments about the revised version of the confession stated that "it is now being published, after having the (original) intent spoiled by a few pastors."[37] The intent of the first version of the Bethel Confession was largely directed by Bonhoeffer himself with the help of George Merz (1892-1959).[38] On justification and the cross, the original confession stated, "the church teaches that godless humankind can find its way to a merciful God only through faith in Jesus Christ, who was crucified and resurrected as intermediary for us."[39] On the Holy Spirit, the original confession stated,

> The church teaches that the Holy Spirit, true God for all eternity, is not created, not made, but proceeds from the Father and the Son; that the Spirit is given to humankind only through the external Word and the sacraments

of the church; that through the Spirit those persons are drawn from all nations whom God has chosen, who will belong to Christ's church; that the Spirit teaches, judges, punishes, and creates faith, conversion, and renewal in human beings.[40]

The early version of the Bethel Confession represented biblical Christianity, which shows not only the reason for Bonhoeffer's frustration with the changes made to the document but also Bonhoeffer's commitment to orthodoxy in wanting such confessional truths to stay intact in the Confessing Church. However, Bonhoeffer's exit from the project when he took up the pastorate in London kept him from having the same level of influence he had originally. Bonhoeffer saw a worrying shift in the spirit of the Confessing Church.

COMMUNITY OF A DIFFERENT SPIRIT

The spirit of the age in 1933 Germany was an ever darkening one. Though many in the church had given in to the political and cultural shifts of the day, Bonhoeffer did not. Though many were participating in such a culturally driven community in the church, Bonhoeffer was not. Later, in *Life Together*, he would write, "Christian community is a spiritual and not a psychic reality."[41] Christian community is created by the Holy Spirit, not by man. Geffrey Kelly has explained Bonhoeffer's contrast between spiritual and psychic as being similar to the apostle Paul's distinction between Spirit and flesh.[42] This is a further argument against man's actions in the creation of Christian community. Christian community is Spirit-created, not flesh-created. Yet, Bonhoeffer's declaration is also a statement about the Holy Spirit's involvement in the Christian community as well as the spiritual nature of Christian community. For Bonhoeffer, thinking about Christian community during a dark age was like stepping into another world, which served as a mental retreat from the bleak picture of reality that surrounded him.

Community created by the Holy Spirit has the truth of the Scriptures as its foundation. The Word of God rules spiritual community. Any other type of community finds itself based on the fallen aspirations of humans. Such community is characterized by darkness, while community made by the Spirit is full of light. The two types of community Bonhoeffer described find their footing either on Jesus Christ or on the wishful dreams of the members. Bonhoeffer linked the Holy Spirit with Jesus as both being inextricably involved and serving their appropriate roles in a proper Christian community. Therefore, Christian community is in Christ by the Spirit.[43]

Usually, we can only see the health of our churches when we look backward. When we begin to reflect back on time gone by and think through where decisions have led us, can we begin to get a sense of whether our church is led by the Spirit in the Word. In other words, we can see the kind of fruit we are producing. Is it good fruit or bad fruit? The Lord Jesus said, "So, every healthy tree bears good fruit, but the diseased tree bears bad fruit. A healthy tree cannot bear bad fruit, nor can a diseased tree bear good fruit. Every tree that does not bear good fruit is cut down and thrown into the fire. Thus you will recognize them by their fruits" (Matt 7:17-20). This kind of fruit-focused assessment can be healthy, to determine where the church may need to get back on track and to determine how to pray. However, we can go too far with this in that all this objectivity may breed discontentment or bitterness in us. Bonhoeffer warns, "Just as Christians should not be constantly feeling the pulse of their spiritual life, so too the Christian community has not been given to us by God for us to be continually taking its temperature."[44]

This can become a kind of navel-gazing that itself does not produce anything healthy. So, we must find a healthy balance in our desire for health as we humbly recognize our weaknesses and shortcomings.

Bonhoeffer has already said that Christian community is through Christ, thus making him its creator. He has also stated that Christian community is a divine reality, that is, something that God has done in advance or has done before any human activity or cooperation. Bonhoeffer explained, "It means ... that from eternity we have been chosen in Jesus Christ, accepted in time, and united for eternity."[45] Bonhoeffer roots Christian community in God's election, pointing to God's sovereign decree of salvation through Christ to be applied by the Holy Spirit. Looking back to Bonhoeffer's description of the involvement of the Holy Spirit in Christian community in *Sanctorum Communio*, Charles Marsh helpfully explained, "The Holy Spirit dwelling in the church is actualized by revelation in Christ; therefore the Spirit does not reside independently of the church."[46] Marsh went on to state Bonhoeffer's position even more succinctly, "Pneumatology is based strictly on christology."[47] Thus, the spiritual nature of Christian community is founded on Christ being the center and the giver of his Spirit to the community.

ELEMENTS OF SPIRITUAL AND EMOTIONAL COMMUNITY

In *Life Together*, Bonhoeffer contrasted spiritual community with psychic, fleshly, or emotional community. Bonhoeffer saw these two kinds of community, spiritual and emotional, as another way to contrast the kind of Christ-centered, biblically sound community we have been speaking about with preference-driven, people-focused community. Spiritual community, which is built on Christ by the Spirit, produces rightly ordered love. Emotional community lacks the resources, namely Christ and his Spirit, to create spiritual love. This kind of love comes from Jesus and is displayed in the Word. The Word drives and defines what this love is. Love in a spiritual community works itself out through the mediation of Christ. This spiritual love allows Jesus to work in the lives of others, because it is only Jesus who has, can, and will work in them. Practically, spiritual love deals in the currency of the Word and prayer.[48] Bonhoeffer contrasts the two kinds of community by showing their differences in terms of timing, how conversion works, and what loves looks like.

Bonhoeffer taught that emotional community, the community not built on Christ by the Spirit, distorts true Christian community. First, emotional community expects immediacy. All things in emotional community must happen right away, including relationships. Second, emotional community has its own type of conversion experience. A person is simply conquered by the whims of others in the community rather than being won over as in true conversion. Bonhoeffer refers to this emotional *conversion* as though such people are won over by other people's perspectives and opinions rather than being won over by the gospel. Third, emotional community has its own way of loving one's neighbor. This type of love serves itself, not Christ.[49]

The difference between emotional community driven by human ideals and spiritual community created by God's reality comes down to the discernment of believers. Emotional community and human ideals are likely to surface even within a Christ-centered community. However, the onus is on those in the community to rightly understand what Christian community should be and to apply the disciplines a Christian community needs to maintain and bring it to maturity.[50] It is to these disciplines that Bonhoeffer turned for much of *Life Together*. We will consider those disciplines in chapter six. It would be helpful to take a closer look at the elements of timing, conversion, and love in both of these types of communities.

For emotional community, *the first element to consider is immediacy*. One does not have to look far in contemporary society to see an urge for immediacy. So many things are designed to shorten waiting times, to make things go faster, to quickly complete tasks, and to deliver things almost instantaneously. The thought of having to wait too long for something to download or to stand in line for anything feels nearly outrageous to many. As Ferris Bueller has said, "Life moves pretty fast. If you don't stop and look around once in a while, you could miss it." Such expectations of immediacy have crept into other aspects of life, not to mention church life. Certain aspects of church growth are expected to happen quickly. Spiritual progress should be noticeable after a few short weeks. Those who are to lead are ready and seasoned almost immediately after feeling a sense of call on their lives. A community burdened by such expectations is driven by human desires. For example, it can be a great temptation to grow impatient when new ministries are started in our churches or when new churches are started. Members and attenders want to see the results soon or they want to experience the benefits of a new teaching ministry right away. But all of those things take time for them to be their best. Bonhoeffer said, "At the foundation of all psychic, or emotional, reality are the dark, impenetrable urges and desires of the human soul."[51] Fallen desires produce expectations of immediacy.

In spiritual community, immediacy is not the standard. Relationships are not expected to simply spring up out of nowhere. Growth in the Christian community is not expected overnight. Christian community is based on God's timetable and not man's. As one of my pastors used to always say, "God is never in a hurry." Spiritual community is not self-centered. It is community mediated through Christ and he decides the speed at which anything happens in his community. So that new ministry that has been thought through and prayed through for months or maybe years may not be too slow to get off the ground, but it needs that time for God to fashion it and all who are involved as he intends.

The second element of emotional community is that it has its own conversion experience. Bonhoeffer describes, "It has all the appearances of genuine conversion and occurs wherever the superior power of one person is consciously or unconsciously misused to shake to the roots and draw into its spell an individual or a whole community. The result is that the weak individual has been overcome by the strong ... One has been overpowered by something, but not won over."[52] Unity in the emotional community is like one's entrance into that community—it happened by coercion. It can be like many of the things of which you may be involved, you said *yes* because you were voluntold or guilted into joining. Another common entry point to such communities is good, old-fashioned peer pressure—everybody is doing this and so should you! Guilt and peer pressure as a means of getting people to take part do not belong in the Lord's church. Such conversion was not brought about by the Holy Spirit and does not last.[53]

In contrast, one's conversion into spiritual community happens by none other than the Holy Spirit. As the apostle Peter preached on the day of Pentecost and people responded to his sermon he instructed them, "Repent and be baptized every one of you in the name of Jesus Christ for the forgiveness of your sins, and you will receive the gift of the Holy Spirit" (Acts 2:38). A response of repentance and faith is the entrance into spiritual community, not coercion by a stronger, more opinionated person or group. Therefore, entrance into this spiritual community has the only true conversion experience. Anything other than a Holy Spirit-wrought repentance and faith is not true conversion. We do not follow the Great Commission (see Matt 28:19-20) by manipulating and coercing people into God's kingdom, instead we go as heralds of the King's message of peace and reconciliation through his Son.

The third element of emotional community is emotional love. Bonhoeffer's way of expressing that should not be confused with the love that one has along with emotional responses. Rather, emotional love is the kind of love that springs from emotional or fleshly community. It is also the kind of love that creates emotional or fleshly community. Bonhoeffer also refers to this love as self-centered love. He makes several important distinctions about this self-centered love. First, such love has an aversion to truth and thereby makes truth relative, so the truth can never get in the way of bringing about one's satisfaction.[54] Furthermore, emotional love would not allow a community to be dissolved or disciplined should it stray from the truth. Emotional love wants to maintain community at any cost for the sake of the individual's desires.[55] Second, Bonhoeffer stated, "Emotional, self-centered love desires other persons, their company. It wants them to return its love, but it does not serve them. On the contrary, it continues to desire even when it seems to be serving."[56] The lack of service is a telltale sign of this kind of love. Third, emotional or self-centered love seeks to make people into one's own image, dictating how another person should be.[57] Finally, Bonhoeffer states, "Self-centered love results in human enslavement, bondage, rigidity."[58] One can look at the product of something to truly know its value; self-centered love, according to Bonhoeffer, does not produce good fruit.

"Spiritual love", Bonhoeffer says, "however, comes from Jesus Christ; it serves him alone."[59] Such love desires not to serve self, but Christ. Bonhoeffer went on to definitively say, "Only Christ in his Word tells me what love is. Contrary to all my own opinions and convictions, Jesus Christ will tell me what love for my brothers and sisters really looks like."[60] Such Christ-dictated love is not averse to the truth but rather is a celebration of it. Spiritual love joyfully serves the other for the sake of the Lord Jesus. Spiritual love longs to see people made into the image of Christ. Therefore, spiritual love creates fruit that lasts and pleases God.

HEAVENLY REALITIES JUST AN IDEAL?

Perhaps you're thinking, "Bonhoeffer's declarations about spiritual community seem to be a bit idealistic. Is it really possible to have community entirely devoid of the elements of emotional community?" Bonhoeffer assumed you would be thinking that. First, it is helpful to remember that while Bonhoeffer is talking about Christian community as essentially being church life, he is also referring to specific experiences of Christian communal life. He experienced this communal life with the students he taught and lived within his underground seminary, which the next chapter will fully discuss. Keeping in mind that Bonhoeffer referred both to life in a local church as well as in smaller communities of Christians is important when considering his arguments. Second, Bonhoeffer understood that even Christian communal life should still be under the auspices of the church: "In other words, a life together under the Word will stay healthy only when it does not form itself into a movement, an order, a society, a *collegium pietatis* (an association of piety), but instead understands itself as being part of the one, holy, universal, Christian church, sharing through its deeds and suffering in the hardships and struggles and promise of the whole church."[61] Third, Bonhoeffer knew that the congregation of sinners in the Christian community is bound to bring elements of emotional community into the spiritual community.[62] Bonhoeffer was willing to admit that Christian community can be messy, complicated, and sometimes difficult, but it takes ongoing work by the congregation to keep the focus on God's reality for Christian community. Therefore, Bonhoeffer's willingness to tip his hat at the likelihood of the complexities of Christian community means that he was not contradicting his warning against idealism.

One could say that the real danger lies in pragmatism. For example, we may be let down if we come to Bonhoeffer's proposal for Christian community with the question: *Does it work?* It is possible in our search for a healthy Christian community we have been rifling through different methods like cards in a Rolodex, trying to find the method that works. Bonhoeffer seems less interested in what works and more interested in what is true. In other words, he wanted to focus on what Christian community should look like according to God rather than trying to discover what brings people together. Such an emphasis is displayed in his consistent Christ-centered theme. It is now displayed in his emphasis on the Holy Spirit actualizing the triune God's reality of union with the Lord Jesus for his people. *That* is what is true. God the Father is bringing together all his people in God the Son by God the Holy Spirit (see Eph 1:1–14). Such a breathtaking statement is descriptive of how God understands Christian community. Why would anyone simply clamor after *what works* after hearing such glorious news? Bonhoeffer said, "It is not the experience of Christian community, but firm and certain faith within Christian community that holds us together."[63] Faith in what is *true* is what will facilitate God's reality in Holy

Spirit-wrought community. Faith in Christ will produce the kind of fruit that God desires in the spiritual community.

SERVICE: A KEY TO SPIRITUAL COMMUNITY

Service is a key fruit that Bonhoeffer describes in *Life Together*. Bonhoeffer has already dealt with the necessity of loving others in the Christian community, but he devoted an entire chapter of *Life Together* to service. Here he was more explicit in how this service was to be rendered. He began with a scene from Luke's Gospel: "An argument started among the disciples as to which of them would be the greatest" (Luke 9:46, Bonhoeffer's translation).[64] The disciples were busy deciding who was most important among them as they walked with Jesus. Bonhoeffer pointed out that this type of attitude is detrimental to community. He also acknowledged the natural tendency people have to compare themselves to those around them. The discord the disciples experienced as a result of their comparison and pride can quickly arise in any Christian community.[65]

Bonhoeffer issued a call to service by focusing on a theme one might not expect. The first service Bonhoeffer said a community can provide to one another starts with the discipline of the tongue. "Let no evil talk come out of your mouths, but only what is useful for building up, as there is need, so that your words may give grace to those who hear" (Eph 4:29 NRSV). Bonhoeffer believed practicing such self-control in one's speech makes way for a breakthrough in community.[66]

> God did not make others as I would have made them. God did not give them to me so that I could dominate and control them, but so that I might find the Creator by means of them. Now other people, in the freedom with which they were created, become an occasion for me to rejoice,

whereas before they were only a nuisance and trouble for me. God does not want me to mold others into the image that seems good to me, that is, into my own image. Instead, in their freedom from me God made other people in God's own image. I can never know in advance how God's image should appear in others.[67]

Such a community looks for its justification by grace not in justifying itself. There is therefore no room for pride but only humility in such a community.[68]

Learning how to serve others must begin with humility: "[You should] not...think of yourself more highly than you ought to think" (Rom 12:3 NRSV). According to Bonhoeffer, this kind of thinking can only come from considering oneself in light of what Christ has done. It is a kind of gospel-informed self-awareness. This will allow people in a community to prioritize others above themselves both in their honor and their will.[69] "What does it matter if I suffer injustice? Would I not have deserved even more severe punishment from God if God had not treated me with mercy?"[70] Only this kind of thinking can come from and be maintained by the grace of Jesus Christ. Christians must align themselves with how Paul thought of himself in his first letter to Timothy: "Christ Jesus came into the world to save sinners—of whom I am the foremost" (1 Tim 1:15 NRSV).

Bonhoeffer also outlined three ways Christians can serve one another according to the Scriptures. The first is listening. How Christians listen to one another and the attitudes they have with one another can be directly related to how they listen to God and the attitude they have toward God.[71] In other words, one's view of God impacts one's view of others. If people are unwilling to listen to God and are unwilling to show him respect, they will likely be the same way toward other people. The second way

Christians can serve one another is through what Bonhoeffer called "active helpfulness."[72] "We must be ready to allow ourselves to be interrupted by God, who will thwart our plans and frustrate our ways time and again, even daily, by sending people across our path with their demands and requests."[73] When the phone call comes late at night from a person in need, we must be willing to set all of our plans, like getting more sleep, to the side. The third kind of service is in bearing one another's burdens. Because Christ suffered for and bore the burdens of humans, believers in Christ can bear other's burdens and so "fulfill the law of Christ" (Gal 6:2).[74] Part of the burden that believers carry for others is because of the freedom others have. The freedom of the other may at times infringe on one's own freedom. The greatest way this freedom impacts the community is when others sinfully abuse their freedom. Yet this is part of bearing with others, namely bearing with the sin of others. This does not call Christians to be doormats, and this does not excuse away the despicable nature of extreme sins like physical and sexual abuse. Instead, Bonhoeffer is talking about all the little things that can eat away at us in community: comments, glances, disappointments, and the like. Service in bearing with others' sin is offering forgiveness.[75]

All service rendered in a Christian community is based on the Word, yet the greatest service that Christians can offer others is serving them with the Word. Serving others with the Word happens as each person gives the Word to another. Serving others with the Word is connected with the other ways of serving. This can happen in Bible studies as we share with each other what God is teaching us as we read and study. This can happen when we spend one-on-one time with a new believer and we show them how to read and understand the Bible. This can happen as we have little encounters in the foyer after service and we seek to fill our words of encouragement to struggling or suffering Christians with the Scriptures. Much of this is helped by good listening. Listening to others helps shape how we might speak the Word back to them. Serving others tangibly is informed by our understanding and appropriation of the Word. Bearing with others may require God's Word to be spoken to them. This assumes that believers allow others to speak God's Word to them. Such scenarios become especially challenging when someone is in sin, yet God's Word must be spoken to those in sin. To avoid doing so is to deny them of God's grace. The Christian community is one marked by a collective desire to come under the obedience of the Word of God.[76]

In essence, the way Bonhoeffer described a Christian community throughout *Life Together* is grounded in the importance of serving others. He writes this way because service is central to the biblical pattern of the Christian life. He described how Christians serve one another through corporate spiritual disciplines. Yet, in his chapter on service, Bonhoeffer discussed both corporate and private spiritual disciplines as means of service to others. There are three elements to note from this chapter. The first is Bonhoeffer's biblical basis for service. The second is Bonhoeffer's use of the writings of Thomas à Kempis (1380–1471) in describing service. The third is Bonhoeffer's use of the writings of Martin Luther (1483–1546) in his approach to service.

Bonhoeffer began by looking at what Scripture had to say about the discipline of the tongue as a foundation for serving others. Using James 4:11–12 and Ephesians 4:29 as primary texts to call for the discipline of the tongue, Bonhoeffer showed how Christian service requires personal discipline in the one serving.[77] He noted, "Where this discipline of the tongue is practiced right from the start, individuals will make an amazing discovery. They will be able to stop constantly keeping an eye on others, judging them, condemning them, and putting them in their places and thus doing violence to them."[78] Bonhoeffer also pointed to Romans 12 to discuss the necessity of using one's mind and heart in Christian service.[79] Thus, he showed God's desire through the Word that the Christian servant be sanctified. Rather than simply walking through acts of service, Bonhoeffer illustrated a God-honoring approach to service.

Bonhoeffer referred to Thomas à Kempis's book, *The Imitation of Christ*. À Kempis's piety is monastic to be sure, but Bonhoeffer sought to normalize it for Protestants. By using à Kempis as an example, Bonhoeffer was not calling Christians to a monastic life but rather showing them that some practices often considered monastic are simply Christian. The following statement from à Kempis almost sounds like it is from the pen of Bonhoeffer: "Likewise, one cannot remain at peace for long who does not strive to be the least important person in the community, attending to others with humility and love. You have come to serve, not to rule."[80] Had à Kempis and Bonhoeffer been contemporaries, they likely would have found a kindred spirit in the other. In referring to à Kempis, Bonhoeffer exhibited the impact this medieval monastic had on him.

Stephen Nichols has rightly pointed out that Bonhoeffer puts the proclamation of the Word and any exercise of authority as needing to be partnered with all the other forms of service in a Christian community.[81] Bonhoeffer's order of services in a Christian community is derivative of Martin Luther's *The Freedom of a Christian*.[82] In this work, Luther stated,

Although individual Christians are thereby free from all works, they should nevertheless once again "humble themselves" in this freedom, take on "the form of a servant," "be made in human form and found in human vesture," and serve, help, and do everything for their neighbor, just as they see God has done and does with them through Christ. And they should do this freely, having regard for nothing except divine approval.[83]

Luther believed that Christian service is rooted in Christ's justifying grace. This is why Bonhoeffer's framework around service in *Life Together* is so analogous to Luther. Bonhoeffer stated, "Self-justification and judging belong together in the same way that justification by grace and serving belong together."[84] As Nichols described, "Bonhoeffer stresses the need for authentic Christian living before the action of proclamation."[85] Thus, the Christian life of one who proclaims the gospel strengthens the effectiveness of the gospel message to the hearer. Such an approach to service in a Christian community is decidedly biblical and Christlike. Just as Bonhoeffer the chaplain was adamant to serve his difficult students, thus he commended the great need for service to mark a true spiritual community.

CONCLUSION

The practical way a Christian community is maintained by God is through the ministry of the Holy Spirit. Many ideas and concepts can lead a group of people, but Christian community must be led by the Lord. He does this by his Spirit through the Word. Christians submit to this leadership with a spirit of humility, looking to the Scriptures. A Christian community works to avoid being swept up into opinions and human perspectives. It follows the Lord and desires to please him alone.

CHAPTER 6

Community in and of the Word

My dear Dietrich, I don't want to let you go without saying a final greeting to you. My prayers will accompany you on your way, and the joy will be very great when you return home. This certainty will always stand by you, when perhaps sometimes in foreign lands it does become very lonely. What you have meant to me is another story, but I believe you know that you have helped me on the path to God. That is what constitutes my special gratitude and my close attachment, something of value that will not die.[1]

On May 31, 1939, the widow of a German aristocrat, Ruth von Kleist (1867–1945), wrote to Bonhoeffer as he prepared to leave for a short trip to America. Bonhoeffer's friendship with this dear saint had begun as he was leading the underground seminary at Finkenwalde. In 1935, Ruth von Kleist, along with her grandchildren, began regularly attending worship services at Finkenwalde. Bonhoeffer grew very close to von Kleist, as her letter portrays. After some time, Bonhoeffer would disciple a few of her grandchildren to their confirmation.[2]

One of those grandchildren, Maria von Wedemeyer (1924–1977), would later become Bonhoeffer's fiancée.[3] One biographer notes the importance of von Kleist not only to Bonhoeffer, but also to the seminary at Finkenwalde:

> After a tour of the seminary, she arranged for the delivery of furniture, rugs, musical instruments, and a variety of other appointments, which she insisted the house needed. Concerned that Bonhoeffer himself lacked a proper work space for his writing, she converted two rooms in her nearby Restow estate into a guest suite and studio.[4]

It is remarkable to consider the impact such a woman of God had on the little Confessing Church seminary at Finkenwalde. She was not only a patroness of the seminary but herself a recipient of the ministry of the Word therein. She served the Lord by supporting those who would serve the Lord in the pastorate. As she served, she worshipped the Lord Jesus with a community in and of the Word.

FINKENWALDE

When Bonhoeffer left London in 1934, he would say openly that he was headed back to Germany to become the director of a Confessing Church preachers' seminary in Düsseldorf, Germany. However, there was no Confessing Church preachers' seminary in Düsseldorf. The location was changed in his public mentions to throw off the Gestapo (Nazi secret police). They were a threat because the Confessing Church seminaries were considered illegal. The actual location of the seminary was in the village of Zingst, in the province of Pomerania near the Baltic Sea. They met in the youth holiday camp owned by the Westphalian School Bible Club for the first two months.[5] On April 26, 1935, Bonhoeffer arrived with his first class of students. They soon found a house in the small country town of Finkenwalde for the seminary's more permanent location.[6] The house needed some refurbishing, which was finished in June 1935.

All the events in Germany thus far had culminated at this moment for Bonhoeffer. His life, in congruence with the political upheaval impacting the church in which he served, brought him to Finkenwalde. Others were brought to Finkenwalde due to the same providential scenarios. What took place in those years in Pomerania were not in a vacuum, insulated from the issues inherent to Germany at large and the world itself, nevertheless a certain serenity seems to emerge from Bonhoeffer's seminary. In those two years, Bonhoeffer would live out many of the themes that were building in his personal life, in his writing, and his ministry.

The first official session of the seminary began in August. Bonhoeffer structured the days for the students in a monastic style, following a schedule that incorporated individual and corporate spiritual disciplines.[7] The seminary continued through the end of 1937 when it was shut down under a decree issued by Heinrich Himmler (1900–45).[8] Eberhard Bethge, who became Bonhoeffer's closest friend and eventual biographer, was one of the seminary students. In July 1936, Confessing Church pastors began getting arrested for associating with non-Nazi churches and organizations. Even Bonhoeffer's students at Finkenwalde were targeted.[9] The oppressive assault the Nazis brought against dissenters like those in the Confessing Church drove Bonhoeffer to be creative with how he continued to educate pastors. Thankfully, Finkenwalde was able to exist for nearly two years and in that time, Bonhoeffer's theology was ripening and bearing fruit.

During these two years, Bonhoeffer worked on two writing projects that have become his most well-known classics. *The*

Cost of Discipleship came from lectures he delivered at the seminary and had been stirring in him for some time. He finished the book shortly before the Gestapo shut down the seminary at Finkenwalde. The finalized copies of *The Cost of Discipleship* were completed during Advent 1937 and some of the first were sent by Bonhoeffer to his former Finkenwalde students.[10] Additionally, an early form of *Life Together* was delivered as lectures at the seminary. Not only were lectures given regarding this content, but the students essentially lived *Life Together* during their time at Finkenwalde.[11]

Geffrey Kelly has said that the Finkenwalde experience had its beginnings in Bonhoeffer's time teaching at the University of Berlin. Bonhoeffer had given a series of lectures titled, "The Nature of the Church," where he expounded on themes present in *Sanctorum Communio*.[12] In these lectures, Bonhoeffer's emphasis on community in the church is a refrain prevalent throughout. In one of the lectures, after asking whether the church is needed, not only did he answer in the affirmative, but he went on to emphatically say, "Community is necessary."[13] Bonhoeffer heavily emphasized the need for community, but he was careful not to divorce it from its *telos* (end or goal) in Christ. His view of the church, according to Kelly, was to be "the community of Jesus Christ that is within the world, yet free enough from the world to oppose secular idolatries and to do the courageous deeds required in serving others."[14] For Bonhoeffer, not only did the church have a purpose to be in community, but the community itself was to have a purpose.

Several of the students who first heard these lectures on "The Nature of the Church" at the University of Berlin in the summer of 1932 joined Bonhoeffer in Finkenwalde.[15] They benefited from the education of the seminary but also in its life. By the autumn of 1935, it became clear that Bonhoeffer was modeling a lifestyle for the students. Bethge explained how Bonhoeffer began to talk about the possibility of a purposeful Christian community late in the summer with his first round of students. By September of that year, an official proposal was drafted and sent to the administrative council over the seminary.[16] The proposal began with the following, "For several years now I, together with several younger brothers whose names appear below, have considered establishing a Protestant House of Brethren in which we wish as pastors to lead a communal Christian life."[17] Bethge was part of the first group of students to commit to living in the House of Brethren and he signed the proposal along with Bonhoeffer. Bethge described the experience as being similar, in parts, to a monastic style of living, without going quite that far. Though there was hesitation on the part of the council to grant permission for Bonhoeffer to establish such a community, given its similarities to Roman Catholic practices and the urgent need for young theologians in the church, he received his permission.[18]

The House of Brethren and the Finkenwalde seminary experience was something of an anomaly, even among the Confessing Church. Charles Marsh explained the way that Bonhoeffer's seminary was viewed by some from the outside:

> While Finkenwalde operated within the ecclesial structures of the German Protestant Church, the decision to study with Bonhoeffer carried real risks. Only two months after classes began, the Old Prussian Union Council decided that the Confessing Church might call itself a "confessional movement" or "confessional front," but it did not have the legitimate status of *Kirche* (church). Thus study with Bonhoeffer became a badge of dissent, and in the eyes of the church authorities it was to mark oneself out as a "radical fanatic" and a disloyal German.[19]

Despite any negative views about what was happening at Finkenwalde, Bonhoeffer continued with what he viewed as his calling—both to teach and live out his convictions.

The day-to-day life at Finkenwalde is best described in *Life Together* itself. However, Paul R. House gave a fitting description of what Bonhoeffer was seeking to do at Finkenwalde:

> His first goal was to form a community on proper grounds. This community would be like the one Jesus formed with his disciples, described in *The Cost of Discipleship*. It would exist to shape shepherds who in turn help churches develop into communing brothers and sisters in Christ. Daily worship, prayer, and meditation were means of shaving off remaining edges of selfishness, ambition, wrongheaded individualism, and theological arrogance.[20]

Such a view of seminary education was countercultural to the norms of that time, but Bonhoeffer saw the long-term potential for good that it could bring. Participation in such a learning experience with Bonhoeffer, as has been stated, was a calculated risk. After Finkenwalde was shut down, Bonhoeffer wrote to his former students to encourage them in their various vocations, and he mentioned that four of their Finkenwalde brothers were in prison.[21] The reality of the times in which they lived and worked came back to the fore.

Geffrey Kelly stated that the shutting down of Finkenwalde by the Gestapo at the end of 1937 gave way for Bonhoeffer to write *Life Together*, which he was hesitant to do up until then. He wrote the book in late September 1938, while staying at his sister's house with Bethge in Göttingen, Lower Saxony.[22] In a letter Bonhoeffer wrote to Erwin Sutz on September 18, he said, "At the moment I have vacation and am trying to write something. But it goes slowly; I have too much else on my mind."[23] It is unclear what he was referring to that cluttered his thinking. One could assume that it was the burdens of the seminary students now spread out and the heightened tension in the country. Though he had much on his mind, he worked tirelessly and finished the book in four weeks.[24] *Life Together* was first published in 1939 as the sixty-first volume in a series called *Theologische Existenz heute* (Theological Existence Today) and immediately sold well.[25]

After the shutdown of the seminary, Bonhoeffer was able to keep the spirit of Finkenwalde going in limited ways. He began to manage two seminaries, one in Köslin and one in Schlawe, which were both in east Pomerania. Both seminaries existed in houses, similar to the Finkenwalde seminary. Things were much more primitive and occasionally locations had to be changed.[26] Yet, the training of dissenting pastors was able to continue for a time. Regretfully, the Confessing Church was crumbling under the pressure it faced. Orders were given in early 1938 that all Protestant pastors had to swear an oath of allegiance to Hitler on his birthday. Later that year, despite efforts by Bonhoeffer and others to the contrary, many of the Confessing Church pastors swore the oath.[27] The trajectory of the Confessing Church led Bonhoeffer to act, which would eventually pull him away from his experiences in Christian community.

THE DAY TOGETHER

Bonhoeffer devoted an entire chapter in *Life Together* to describing a day in the life of a Christian community. While he spoke of a day with his seminary students, his admonitions could be applied to a weekly rhythm of worship for a church. With an eye toward the early light of the morning, Bonhoeffer quoted Martin Luther's translation of a hymn written by Ambrose of Milan (d. 397) titled "O Blessed Light." He then referenced the apostle Paul's letter to the Colossians: "Let the word of Christ dwell in you richly ..." (Col 3:16 NRSV).[28] This verse captures the essence of the chapter. Bonhoeffer was concerned to show everything that the Word of Christ does amid the Christian community. The Word rules over the day of a Christian community as it lives and worships together.

The day of worship is to have three essential elements to it: Scripture, hymns, and prayer. These elements are all essential parts of monastic life. They are specifically part of the monastic life of the Augustinian order, of which Luther, Bonhoeffer's primary theological forefather, was once a part. Augustinian monks were to take part in various Scripture readings each day, some of which were responsive.[29] Monks of this order were also to give themselves to prayer and to singing hymns.[30] Since these practices are unique to the monastic life, Bonhoeffer's approach appears all the more countercultural.

Christian community together began for Bonhoeffer first thing in the morning. "The early morning belongs to the church of the risen Christ. At the break of light it remembers the morning on which death, the devil, and sin were brought low in defeat, and new life and salvation were given to human beings."[31] Such a truth requires a response of worship from the Christian community. The day begins with worship, and worship begins with the psalms. As in his epistle to the Colossians, Paul calls the Ephesians to, "speak to one another with Psalms" (Eph 5:19, Bonhoeffer's translation).[32]

Bonhoeffer particularly emphasized praying the psalms. He asked the question that many have asked about the psalms: "How can God's Word be at the same time prayer to God?"[33] Yet that is precisely what the Psalms are, God's Word that is to be offered in prayer back to God. Bonhoeffer wrote a small book on the psalms attempting to delve further into this wonderful mystery.

If we want to read and to pray the prayers of the Bible, and especially the Psalms, we must not, therefore, first ask what they have to do with us, but what they have to do with Jesus Christ. We must ask how we can understand the Psalms as God's Word, and only then can we pray them with Jesus Christ. Thus it does not matter whether the Psalms express exactly what we feel in our heart at the moment we pray. Perhaps it is precisely the case that we must pray against our own heart in order to pray rightly. It is not just that for which we ourselves want to pray that is important, but that for which God wants us to pray.[34]

Bonhoeffer picked up this theme in *Life Together* by stating that the psalms are Jesus' prayer for the church. Thus, the church joins Jesus in his prayer when it prays the psalms.[35]

Bonhoeffer argued that praying the psalms teaches prayer. First, praying the psalms shows what prayer is, namely that it is praying on the foundation of God's promises.[36] Second, praying the psalms teaches what should be prayed.[37] Third, praying the psalms teaches how to pray in community.[38] Once the psalms are prayed through in the Christian community, a hymn is sung and the next portion of the day of worship begins.[39]

Bonhoeffer quoted from Paul's first letter to Timothy, "Give attention to the public reading of Scripture ..." (1 Tim 4:13 NRSV). Bonhoeffer pushed against Scripture readings only consisting of brief passages. He gave the examples of the small meditation books printed by the Moravian Brethren or small calendars with a verse or two per day. Though these short devotional readings can be helpful, they are not to be the only intake of Scripture for the church.[40] Bonhoeffer rooted his stance against smaller readings in the way in which Scripture has been given to the church. "The Holy Scriptures do not consist of individual sayings, but are a whole and can be used most effectively as such."[41] Therefore, as with other practices in which the church participates, the public reading of Scripture can be a formative practice, helping the hearers grow and be stretched as they learn how to digest Scripture in its context.

Bonhoeffer suggested the practice of *lectio continua* (continuous reading), wherein books of the Bible are read through consecutively. Such a practice would occur regularly in churches following a lectionary in their liturgy.[42] This practice immerses the congregation into the story unfolding in Scripture. Bonhoeffer stated, "The community of believers is drawn into the Christmas story, the baptism, the miracles and discourses, the suffering, dying, and rising of Jesus Christ."[43] It is Jesus Christ, Bonhoeffer argued, who should hold the church's attention during the reading of Scripture.

> It is in fact more important for us to know what God did to Israel, in God's son Jesus Christ, than to discover what God intends for us today. The fact that Jesus Christ died is more important than the fact that I will die. And the fact that Jesus Christ was raised from the dead is the sole ground of my hope that I, too, will be raised on the day of judgment.[44]

Thus, as is to be expected with Bonhoeffer, the public reading of Scripture for the church was decidedly Christocentric.

Knowing the Scriptures was an important concept for Bonhoeffer. By this, he meant knowing them not just in terms of their content, but so that they were a part of the believer's life and thinking. He called for Christians to know the Scriptures as the Reformers did. Most importantly, that means Christians need to know the Scriptures for salvation. Also, Christians need to know the Scriptures to make significant decisions. Christians need to know the Scriptures to gain confidence in the direction of their lives. Finally, Christians need to know the Scriptures to minister to others who are struggling.[45] For Bonhoeffer, all of these benefits came through the means of the public reading of Scripture.

The last section of his discussion of the public reading of Scripture deals with how it is to be done. He has already advocated for reading longer passages and preferably consecutive readings. He offered additional counsel for the reading of Scripture such as how it should be read: it should be done in a way that directs every hearer's attention to God.[46]

The next significant component of Christians in community together is singing. This practice, Bonhoeffer stated, brings together praying the psalms and the public Scripture reading.[47] The chapter of *Life Together* that discusses this theme of singing is full of quotations from various hymns, both ancient and contemporary, demonstrating Bonhoeffer's love of hymnody and his belief in its value. Also, in keeping with his appreciation for the psalms, he quoted a familiar refrain from them, "O sing to the Lord a new song ..." (Ps 96:1 NRSV). As music is a type of crescendo of worship and thanksgiving, Bonhoeffer presents it as the right response to the Word.

Bonhoeffer presents the order of worship as he does with a purpose. The response of singing follows the Word, and Bonhoeffer argued that there were a few prerequisites to singing properly. There should be a dedication to the Word. The community of Christians should be bound together in Christ, and all parts of the community should be included. Each member of the community should exhibit humility in singing. This means that there needed to be a healthy self-awareness in communal singing, so as to not drown others out and to recognize the importance of singing together. Finally, discipline should characterize the entire approach of congregational singing. Essentially, the spirit of Paul's words to the Corinthian church ought to rule singing: "But all things should be done decently and in order" (1 Cor 14:40). Bonhoeffer returned to Ephesians 5:19 to summarize what takes place in congregational singing.[48]

Having approached it from a spiritual perspective, he made some interesting comments about singing in unison, which were meant to be practical. Bonhoeffer himself was an accomplished musician such that earlier in life he thought he might pursue music professionally.[49] It is from his musical sensibility that he called out things that can be hostile to such singing. Bonhoeffer found no place for those that want to draw attention to themselves in congregational singing either through the boisterous display of their talents, their lack of self-awareness to discern that they have no talent to boast about, or not being willing to participate. Each of these things, says Bonhoeffer, can be harmful to God-honoring congregational singing.[50] To be sure, Bonhoeffer's opinions here can seem a bit jarring. His comments partly show his own personality; he was a bit of a perfectionist and he had high expectations of others. Also, we see his own musical sensibilities coming through his comments. What can be gained from his perspective is the earlier point about humility. Some of us were not gifted with melodious singing voices this side of glory, yet we still sing praises to God. Some of us were so gifted and as we sing with other brothers and sisters, we claim no superiority over others, because our ability is from God, not from ourselves. We should say with the psalmist, "Let everything that has breath praise the LORD!" (Ps 150:6a).

The next portion of the day together is corporate prayer. Having already prayed the psalms together, this type of prayer in Christian community looks different. Bonhoeffer began by quoting Jesus from Matthew's Gospel. "If two of you agree about anything you ask for, it will be done for you by my Father in heaven" (Matt 18:19, Bonhoeffer's translation).[51] For Bonhoeffer to refer to this verse shows something about how he looks at this type of prayer, namely that it is something the community does together. Yet, that does not simply mean just the practice of praying, but the things for which the congregation prays. The struggle with this prayer comes because it is in the people's own words. Unlike praying the psalms, this prayer is free, made up of the words of the people, and is spoken back to God.[52] Yet, one could argue that this prayer is not free, because it has followed the praying of the psalms, the public reading of Scripture, and the congregational singing in the flow of worship. Thus, this prayer is informed by what has already occurred in the community in and around the Word.

An important aspect of the prayer for the Christian community is that it is the prayer of the community. Bonhoeffer was careful to distinguish that this prayer is not that of the individual, but of the community. This presupposes that such praying individuals are a part of the community and thus know what to pray. Knowledge of the community and its needs is essential. For those new to the faith or new to the group or congregation, there must be a learning curve. One can learn through Scripture the general things that Christians are to pray for one another by looking at the prayers of Paul in his letters or at the Lord's Prayer. One can also seek to grow in fellowship with the people to know their needs. Yet, this time of joining in this prayer as a new person can be another great way of learning prayer, by listening to the prayers of others. Furthermore, those praying for the community need the prayer of other individuals of the community to rightly pray for the community.[53]

Praying for the community is a responsibility. Bonhoeffer argued against passing off this duty because someone feels unfit for it. This might be the case for a new believer or for someone fighting sin in their lives. This is an opportunity for the person tasked to pray to know the duty of serving their community in this way. Also, the community should be relied upon to uphold in prayer the one praying for them.[54]

Bonhoeffer dealt with two scenarios involving corporate prayer. The first is the question of whether to use set prayers or not. Bonhoeffer stated that they can be a help, but they can also be a disservice to prayer. Relying on set prayers could be a way in which the church deceives itself about the quality of their prayer life. Bonhoeffer is speaking from within a certain church background where set prayers were more common. Different church traditions have different perspectives on set prayers. His general point is that making anything too routine can eventually lack real spiritual vitality. Second, Bonhoeffer grappled with the helpfulness of special prayer groups. Such a group should not be sought after by force nor as a means of divisiveness. In other words, a special prayer group should not be an exclusive group meant to separate some.[55]

The next aspect of Christian life together is the breaking of bread. Bonhoeffer stated that God's Word and the worship it provokes comes before breaking bread. He referred to the disciples on the road to Emmaus with Jesus in Luke's Gospel, wherein they ended the day at table with Jesus.[56]

> The Scriptures speak of three kinds of community at the table that Jesus keeps with his own: the daily breaking of bread together at meals, the breaking of bread together at the Lord's Supper, and the final breaking of bread together in the reign of God. But in all three, the one thing that counts is that "their eyes were opened and they recognized him."[57]

For Bonhoeffer, in each of these events, the Christian is called to recognize Jesus as the giver, to know all that is received is for the sake of Jesus, and to be assured of Jesus's desire to be present with his people.[58] The breaking of bread is a regular reminder of celebration and rest in the Lord. Also, for the community of Christians, the breaking of bread invokes a responsibility to act as a community and share the common bread the Lord provides.[59]

A final element of a day of Christian life together is work. Bonhoeffer balanced work and prayer explaining that one cannot exist without the other. Work provides opportunities for prayer and prayer empowers work. In attempting to show how work ultimately serves God, Bonhoeffer developed a path from work to the fulfillment of Paul's exhortation to the church in Colossae.[60] "And whatever you do, in word or deed, do everything in the name of the Lord Jesus ... " (Col 3:17, Bonhoeffer's translation).[61] Bonhoeffer wanted Christians to embrace their work in the world for God and to rely on his strength through prayer.[62]

Bonhoeffer closed the chapter by walking through the order of the day. The time of worship and prayer in the morning serves the day of work. If possible, Christians gather at midday for a brief period of rest. Finally, at the close of the day, Christians in life together gather again for worship. Thus, the Christian community acknowledges the Lord's sovereignty over the day and them as his people.[63]

ANALYZING THE DAY TOGETHER

There are several notable things about Bonhoeffer's portrayal of a Christian community's day together. First, the chapter that discusses it, is the longest in *Life Together*. In comparison with the chapter that follows it, which talks about individual worship, one could surmise that Bonhoeffer put a greater emphasis on corporate worship over and above private worship. Second, the chapter is deeply biblical. Nearly seventy times Bonhoeffer either quoted, alluded to or mentioned passages of Scripture. Third, it is deeply doxological. Bonhoeffer directly quoted and referred to several hymns from various periods of church history. Thus, he described various aspects of corporate worship in a Christian community. Lastly, it is deeply ecclesiological. Though the book is written to describe communal Christian living, the practices that Bonhoeffer described should be part of regular church life.

The first characteristic of this chapter worth investigating further is the abundance of biblical references. Some have claimed that Bonhoeffer's view of the Bible fell short of a contemporary evangelical view of the Bible.[64] Due to Bonhoeffer's friendship with Karl Barth, some have assumed Bonhoeffer's view of the Bible to be synonymous with Barth's. It is commonly thought that Barth saw Scripture as witnessing to divine revelation rather than Scripture itself being divine revelation.[65] To be sure, this is an important distinction. However, those who claim Bonhoeffer had such a view of the Bible seem to have him wrong. At least, they have the Bonhoeffer of *Life Together* wrong. Of the Bible, Bonhoeffer said, "It is God's revealed Word for all peoples, for all times. ... The Scriptures are God's revealed Word as a whole."[66] That statement is quite clear. Furthermore, Bonhoeffer's use of Scripture throughout *Life Together* displays his belief in its authority. In other words, what the Scriptures say to do in worship, Bonhoeffer commended to be done. Thus, he thought that when Scripture speaks, God speaks.[67] Simply taking Bonhoeffer's writing in *Life Together* and the second chapter particularly, it is evident he held a high view of Scripture.

Another important characteristic of this chapter is its doxological emphasis. Bonhoeffer made extensive use of hymns throughout the chapter and not just in places where he described corporate singing.[68] In the preface to a hymnal of German hymns translated into English, the author writes about the importance of hymnody to the German people from the time of the Reformation and after.[69] Thus, it seems a hardy love for hymns became embedded into the fabric of what it meant to be Lutheran. Bonhoeffer seems to have stood firmly in that tradition. One such hymn he quoted at the start of the chapter is by Johann Heermann (1585–1647). The English translation gave the hymn the title, "Christ Our Champion."[70] Heermann's hymn is an Easter hymn pointing to the finished work of the resurrected Jesus.[71] About this hymn, Bonhoeffer stated, "So sang the church of the Reformation."[72] Bonhoeffer desired to be Christ-centered even in his singing. Some of the other hymns Bonhoeffer mentioned were written by the Bohemian Brethren, a group that left a lasting impact on him.[73] This impact likely stemmed from his mother's time in Herrnhut with the Moravian Brethren when she was younger.[74] Bonhoeffer's upbringing in music, love of hymnody in his theological tradition, and biblical conviction for worship coalesced in a hymn-besotted exhortation to worship. Oh, how the contemporary church needs to sing old and new hymns, write hymns, teach hymns to children, and celebrate theologically rich hymns!

Finally, the last characteristic to note from the second chapter of *Life Together* is the ecclesial nature of the disciplines he espouses. Nothing that Bonhoeffer exhorted his readers to do is outside the realm of normal church practice. At least in the history of the church, he has not suggested a new path of spirituality. Though many saw the practices of Finkenwalde to be odd, praying through psalms, public Scripture reading, singing in unison, and extemporaneous prayer should not have been shocking practices, as they are quite normal from a biblical standpoint. One would not need to look far to find these elements in contemporary churches. They were, or are, perhaps not practiced the same way or more specifically with the same frequency as Bonhoeffer encouraged, nevertheless they can be considered normal church practices. Keeping this in mind negates any view that Bonhoeffer suggested a novel path of spirituality.

A LITURGY OF DISCIPLINES

The prominent elements of *Life Together* that stand out to many contemporary Christians are the ways Bonhoeffer's community was ordered and the way the community engaged in worship. Bonhoeffer's ideal community had a set pattern of worship, and that set pattern was intentionally filled with biblical practices. Another word for that set pattern of worship is liturgy. For many, that word conjures up negative thoughts about formalism and rote, dry practices. The fact is, every church, every Christian community, has a liturgy. Even if the group is more relaxed in their approach, there is an understood pattern of how things will go as the group gathers. A good question to ask is, are the things in that set pattern the things that God wants his church to do? Thankfully, we need not scratch our heads in confusion as to what God wants his church to do, he has made that plain in the Scriptures. Such Bible-commanded practices are often referred to as spiritual disciplines. Disciplines can be either those practiced by individuals or those practiced corporately by the community. Bonhoeffer's community was one immersed in and produced by the Word. This was displayed through his liturgy of disciplines.

Many have heard the saying, "You are what you eat." However, it is also true that we are what we do. James K. A. Smith has convincingly made that argument in his book, *Desiring the Kingdom:*

Worship, Worldview, and Cultural Formation. Smith speaks broadly of liturgies, not just concerning church: "In short, liturgies make us certain kinds of people, and what defines us is what we *love*."[75] Bonhoeffer operates under a similar notion that we become what we worship. In a sermon he once preached on the golden calf incident in Exodus 32, Bonhoeffer made the case that idols are gods fashioned according to human ideals, which both display and shape their worshippers.[76] Therefore, what we worship ought to be the one true God and how we worship him must be as he directs. Bonhoeffer portrays the importance of a biblical liturgy through how he ordered the regular day at Finkenwalde. The things that Bonhoeffer's Christian community did together were forming them into certain kinds of people, thus those things needed to be the right things. While he was training pastors, he was also forming them into certain kinds of Christians, namely those who would take such formation and seek for it to transform others.

Shortly after his time at Finkenwalde, Bonhoeffer wrote a meditation on Psalm 119. Commenting on verse 4, which states, "You have commanded your precepts to be kept diligently," Bonhoeffer said of God's commandments,

> They have a certain purpose, a goal, for me. They are not given for their own sake but for our sake, namely, that we "keep them diligently." We are to hold on to the commandments when they come from God to us, diligently, earnestly, with all our strength, so that they cannot be lost to us or torn away from us. God's commandment is there not only for the moment but permanently. It wants to enter us deeply and wants to be held fast in every condition of life.[77]

Surely, this is the intent of the apostle Paul's words, "Let the word of Christ dwell in you richly, teaching and admonishing one another in all wisdom, singing psalms and hymns and spiritual songs, with thankfulness in your hearts to God" (Col 3:16). The word of Christ dwelling in a community is how God transforms his people. Constructing a biblical liturgy for a Christian community or church ensures the word of Christ has its proper abode within the community.

CONCLUSION

Every culture and age must take the unchanging Scriptures and apply them. Thus, when Bonhoeffer needed to understand and help others around him understand what it meant to be part of a faithful Christian community in his time, he turned to that which does not change: God's Word. There are many riches to unearth from Bonhoeffer's writing on the application of the Word. The discovery of those riches comes through understanding Bonhoeffer and his context. *Life Together* was the culmination of the trajectory of Bonhoeffer's life, ministry, and study. He offered a biblical vision of Christian community that was set up against the pressures he and others faced from the world around him. His theology of Christian community was centered in Jesus Christ because the Christian community is created by Jesus Christ. According to Bonhoeffer, Christian community was to be preserved through regular participation in a set pattern of worship full of biblical practices. This was truly how the word of Christ could and should dwell richly among the church.

CHAPTER 7

A Call to Christian Community

> The community of the holy Lord's Supper is above all the fulfillment of Christian community. Just as the members of the community of faith are united in body and blood at the table of the Lord, so they will be together in eternity. Here the community has reached its goal. Here joy in Christ and Christ's community is complete. The life together of Christians under the Word has reached its fulfillment in the sacrament.[1]

These are beautiful words. For Bonhoeffer, Christian community culminates in the celebration of the Lord's Supper. In a physical act given to the church by the Lord, believers can commune together with their Savior and King. Certainly, Bonhoeffer holds a high view of the sacrament, but various strands of his theological perspectives come together in his understanding of the celebration at the table. First, he notes that Christian community has a purpose, which is to reach its fulfillment in the tangible display of unity in Christ. Second, he affirms union with Christ, which all believers share. Third, the Christian community is characterized by joy in the Lord Jesus.

Finally, Christian community has its foundation in the Word, through which is revealed the Word made flesh. The experience of communion at the table is a taste of the eternal, joyful fellowship all of Christ's people will share forever. Paul reminded the believers in Ephesus of this great plan of God to bring his people together in Jesus,

> In him we have redemption through his blood, the forgiveness of our trespasses, according to the riches of his grace, which he lavished upon us, in all wisdom and insight making known to us the mystery of his will, according to his purpose, which he set forth in Christ as a plan for the fullness of time, *to unite all things in him*, things in heaven and things on earth (Eph 1:7–10).

In Christian community we get a taste of this union and at the table together we get an even sweeter taste.

Bonhoeffer continues to be a guide for us today in our understanding and practice of Christian community. He remains a source of truth and a brother from whom we can learn. Several key takeaways emerge from what has thus far been discussed and I would commend them to you as you process how to put this into practice.

Bonhoeffer shows us that Christian community, to the glory of God in Christ, fulfills the desire we have for belonging and fellowship (see Matt 18:20; Ps 133:1). People generally desire community. Yes, there are some who would rather pull away and refrain from connecting with others, but for the most part, people desire to belong and connect with others. The best part of that desire comes from our creator who said that it is not good for man to be alone. The best fulfillment of that desire also comes from our creator. He has made and invited us into the community of his son. It is in the body of Christ where we will find the belonging and fellowship we long for.

In an early published work, *Creation and Fall*, Bonhoeffer connected Adam's loneliness, Christ's, and our own. He explained that before Eve, Adam was alone. At many times and certainly in his passion, Christ was alone. And we so often find ourselves alone. Bonhoeffer said, "Adam is alone in anticipation of the other person, of community. Christ is alone because he alone loves the other person, because Christ is the way by which the human race has returned to its Creator. We are alone because we have pushed other people away from us, because we have hated them. Adam was alone in hope, Christ was alone in the fullness of deity, we are alone in evil, in hopelessness."[2]

Each has a reason for being alone and are thus alone in different ways. First, before Eve, no suitable helper was found for Adam. He had no human community, which is what Bonhoeffer argued that marriage was for Adam and Eve. Bonhoeffer went on to describe the connection between this marriage community and the church (see Eph 5:22–33). Before the fall, Adam desired what the Lord said he needed—community. Second, Christ was alone, because though he is God with us, there is no one else like him (Pss 35:10a, 50:21b, 71:19b). Only he was suitable to serve as the mediator between God and man (1 Tim 2:5). Finally, we are alone because of sin. Sin harms and ruins relationships (Gen 3–4). Bonhoeffer was clear about the effect sin has on relationships with others. He was clear elsewhere about the effect sin had on people's relationship with God.[3]

Praise God who in Jesus brought about the repair of our broken relationship with God and with others. Not only that, but in Jesus he has restored our desire for community that Adam had before the fall.

Bonhoeffer shows that there is a close connection between our relationship with God and our relationship with God's people. This is well represented in the New Testament (see 1 John). It is also displayed in our experience. Many have expressed that what we really believe as Christians is displayed through how we live with others. God's desire for our lives, both now and in eternity, is that we would be unified in Jesus. God would not lead us as Christians to live in such a way that discounts or fails to care for others. He would also not lead us to avoid the rest of his people; that desire for avoidance or worse yet, a spirit of resentment, may be revealing a relational problem we have with the Lord.

Christian community is hard because we are fallen (and all God's people said, "Amen!"). How difficult community is this side of heaven! Challenges abound, feelings are hurt, opinions are shared, differences arise, and sometimes it just does not seem possible. What if I get hurt again? What if they disappoint me like those other people did? What if I do not fit in? Questions like these can cause us to pull away from community. All creation groans with you at the fact that Christian community and ten thousand other things are hard in this life (see Rom 8:22). May you not grow weary or frustrated at what Bonhoeffer calls us to in Christian community because you struggle to see it in your own experience. Sin has ruined everything. Our own hearts as well as our emotions and thoughts have not escaped the reaches of sin's destruction. You are not crazy, Christian community is hard! But...

Christian community is a good and sure thing because God made it. Once again, our good God has said that it is *not* good for man to be alone, which of course implies that it is good for us to be with others. James has reminded us, "Every good gift and every perfect gift is from above, coming down from the Father of lights, with whom there is no variation or shadow due to change" (Jas 1:17). Our good God gives us good things. Christian community is good. Church is good. These statements are true because God is good. Christian community is worth the toil and the challenges it presents. God would not call us to something harmful or unnecessary. May we trust in his goodness as we press ahead!

Christian community is created and maintained through the ordinary means of grace and the spiritual disciplines. We have established that God is the creator of Christian community, but in time as we are part of community being created, God uses particular means to do that. The means are captured for us in what we often call spiritual disciplines. These are practices found in Scripture that God has prescribed for his people to do. Donald Whitney states, "...the Spiritual Disciplines found in Scripture are *sufficient* for knowing and experiencing God, and for growing in Christlikeness."[4] Knowing God and growing in Christlikeness is precisely what happens in Christian community, and these things are experienced together. So as the Scriptures are preached and taught, and as people pray, Christian community is fostered and maintained. The ministry of the Word and prayer are the ingredients necessary for Christian community to flourish (see Acts 6:4). No other special ingredients exist. Bonhoeffer made this plain as he described the typical day for a Christian community. The ordinary means of grace and the spiritual disciplines are the fuel for the engine of healthy Christian community, whether it be a church or a small group of some kind. Christian community must rely on the Spirit and the Word to stay focused on Jesus and thus be healthy and life-giving.

When we pull the focus away from Jesus in Christian community, we ruin it. This becomes evident as the results of such misplaced focus become apparent. In other words, if a congregation or small group gets its eyes off Jesus, it may take some time for that to be felt. Such shifts often happen slowly and thus their results are seen slowly. If the ordinary means of grace and the spiritual disciplines stop being part of what the church does or small group practices, then the focus will turn away from Jesus. If the group or congregation becomes more focused on the personality of a leader or the happiness of its members, then the focus will turn away from Jesus. When the focus turns away from Jesus the community is in danger of simply being a gathering of people rather than a Christian community. Certainly, a church cannot be called a church if it is not focused on Jesus; at least it cannot be called a Christian church. Keeping our collective eye focused on the Lord Jesus is a key area of Christian community worth protecting.

Those who struggle with community, in general, can find hope in the gospel to reorient their desires and provide healing. Even though Christian community is a good thing from a good God, people still struggle with it. Some bear deep wounds from ways they have been hurt by professing Christians. Some of those hurts are emotional, some of those are physical, and all of them are painful. The gospel is a balm for such pain. The Lord Jesus has borne the wrath of God our sins deserve on the cross. He has suffered for us. He has died for us. He was raised to new life for us. He intercedes for us. He stands with us in our suffering. Jesus is making his people more and more like him by the power of his Spirit through his Word. So, every hurt that you and I have experienced, even from professing Christians, Jesus has seen, he is faithful to give us grace to walk through it, and he will right every wrong. Jesus is also faithful to help us heal this side of heaven so that we might reenter community with his people.

Others who struggle with community may have a difficult time being around others or being around large crowds. You may call it being introverted, you may chalk it up to anxiety, or maybe both. Both of those things are real experiences. Those who have an introverted personality must know that there are God-honoring aspects of our personalities, but also that the fall has tarnished our personalities. This requires us to be discerning and honest with ourselves about those two aspects of who we are. If you tend to be more recharged by having time alone, that is understandable, but if you belong to Jesus, you belong to his body. Dear friend, do not avoid God's good gift to you. If anxiety is a struggle for you, then seek good biblical counseling, preach the gospel to yourself, seek trusted friends who will pray with and for you, and seek appropriate medical care when it is needed. May this struggle not be something that holds you back from the blessing of being with God's people.

There are still others who struggle with Christian community because of a wrong view of friendship. I have heard many people speak favorably about their church saying, "we love it because we have friends there." I have heard others talk about their season of coming to a new church as them desiring to make friends. Sometimes people leave churches because they do not feel like they have any friends. The issue is that we have equated participation in Christian community with friendship. Meaning, we fit into a church if we make friends, and we do not fit into a church if we do not make friends. Real friendships built on mutual faith in Christ are a wonderful blessing, so I am not saying friendship is a problem. Yet, the examples I am giving are not describing such Christ-exalting friendships. They are describing the baseline idea of friendship as whether or not you like the same things as other people and generally get along with them. So, do you see the issue in equating friendship with

participation in Christian community? It is essentially viewing Christian community as social cohesion, as we discussed
in the first chapter. Meaning, if we say that we only fit into a
Christian community if we have friends, then we are saying
that Christian community is based on whether or not we get
along with everyone. Hopefully, if you have received nothing
else from this book, you may have at least been convinced by
Bonhoeffer that such a thing cannot be said of Christian community. Christian community is not just a group of friends in that
basic sense. Bonhoeffer has described Christian community in
a manner helpful to this point, "Our community consists solely
in what Christ has done to both of us." [5] God gets the glory when
two or two hundred people are united together in Christ rather
than because they all think the same, like the same things, or
get along. So have Christ-exalting friendships and pursue them
but know that Christian community is founded on Christ's work
and not our preferences and interests.

I have defined Christian community as *lifelong fellowship with
other believers in Jesus, who won this gift for his people, maintains it
by the Holy Spirit and the Word, and ordains it to be best expressed
in local churches*. The elements present in that definition are
exemplified in Bonhoeffer's work and more importantly, in the
Scriptures. As we allow God's plan for community to steer us in
our day we will be met with challenges and competing claims.
Praise God that we can look back to faithful believers of the past
like Bonhoeffer, who have participated in the ancient tradition
of following Jesus. May God give us grace to learn and strive after
Christ-exalting churches and small groups in our day!

BONHOEFFER'S END AND BEGINNING

We began with Bonhoeffer alone in Tegel military prison in
Berlin, but this was not where things ended for him. He was

first put there after his arrest. He was able to have visitors at Tegel, frequently seeing Maria and his parents. However, as things worsened, he lost his privileges.[6] He remained at Tegel through October 1944. He was moved to the cellar prison of the Reich SS Headquarters. An attempt was made on Hitler's life in July, which caused tensions to rise and thus difficulties for Bonhoeffer.[7] After all, his ties to threats against Hitler was partly why Bonhoeffer was in prison in the first place. In February 1945, Bonhoeffer was transferred to an unknown location and later to the concentration camp in Buchenwald.[8] Two months later on April 9 at Flossenbürg concentration camp, Bonhoeffer, along with five other prisoners "were forced to undress and were led naked down the short steps from the detention barracks to the gallows that had been erected against a high brick wall."[9] Earlier that day, he led the other prisoners in a worship service. One biographer detailed the service, "So Bonhoeffer read the Bible texts for that day, 'With his stripes we are healed' (Isa 53:5) and 'Blessed be the God and Father of our Lord Jesus Christ! By his great mercy we have been born anew to a living hope through the resurrection of Jesus Christ from the dead' (1 Pet 1:3)."[10] Hitler himself seems to have made the decision for both Bonhoeffer and Hans von Dohnanyi to be executed on April 5.[11]

Bonhoeffer left the majority of his belongings to Bethge, including his writings. Bethge was instrumental in getting *Letters and Papers From Prison* published as well as *Ethics*. Bethge was also the one who confirmed the news about the prisoners' deaths and communicated it to their families after his release from prison in late April.[12] A memorial service for Bonhoeffer was held on July 27, 1945, led in part by Bishop George Bell in Holy Trinity Church, Kingsway, London. In his sermon, Bell called Bonhoeffer a martyr.[13] Bonhoeffer was immortalized in a statue carved on the west portal of Westminster Abbey, where he stands holding an open Bible.[14] The life, ministry, and writings of Dietrich Bonhoeffer are a gift of God to the church. He reminds the church of the devotion and courage needed in following Jesus Christ. In that spirit of courageous hope Bonhoeffer deserves the last word, with the last words he was reported to say as he was led to his execution, "This is the end, for me, the beginning of life."[15]

Abbreviations

BECNT   Baker Exegetical Commentary on the New Testament

DBWE 1   Bonhoeffer, Dietrich. *Dietrich Bonhoeffer Works*, English ed. Vol.
           1, *Sanctorum Communio: A Theological Study of the Sociology of
           the Church*. Edited by Clifford J. Green. Translated by Reinhard
           Krauss and Nancy Lukens. Minneapolis: Fortress Press, 1998.

DBWE 3   Bonhoeffer, Dietrich. *Dietrich Bonhoeffer Works*, English ed.
           Vol. 3, *Creation and Fall: A Theological Exposition of Genesis
           1–3*. Edited by Martin Rüter, Ilse Tödt, and John W. de Gruchy.
           Translated by Douglas Stephen Bax. Minneapolis: Fortress
           Press, 2004.

DBWE 4   Bonhoeffer, Dietrich. *Dietrich Bonhoeffer Works*, English ed.
           Vol. 4, *Discipleship*. Edited by Geffrey B. Kelly and John D.
           Godsey. Translated by Barbara Green and Reinhard Krauss.
           Minneapolis: Fortress Press, 2003.

DBWE 5   Bonhoeffer, Dietrich. *Dietrich Bonhoeffer Works*, English ed. Vol.
           5, *Life Together* and *Prayerbook of the Bible*. Edited by Geffrey B.
           Kelly. Translated by Daniel W. Bloesch and James H. Burtness.
           Minneapolis: Fortress Press, 2005

DBWE 8   Bonhoeffer, Dietrich. *Dietrich Bonhoeffer Works*, English ed. Vol.
           8, *Letters and Papers from Prison*. Edited by John W. De Gruchy.
           Translated by Isabel Best, Lisa E. Dahill, Reinhard Krauss, and
           Nancy Lukens. Minneapolis, Fortress Press, 2010.

DBWE 9   Bonhoeffer, Dietrich. *Dietrich Bonhoeffer Works*, English
           ed. Vol. 9, *The Young Bonhoeffer, 1918–1927*. Edited by Paul
           Duane Matheny, Clifford J. Green, and Marshall D. Johnson.

Translated by Mary C. Nebelsick and Douglas W. Scott. Minneapolis: Fortress Press, 2003.

DBWE 10   Bonhoeffer, Dietrich. *Dietrich Bonhoeffer Works,* English ed. Vol. 10, *Barcelona, Berlin, New York, 1928–1931.* Edited by Clifford J. Green. Translated by Douglas W. Scott. Minneapolis: Fortress Press, 2008.

DBWE 11   Bonhoeffer, Dietrich. *Dietrich Bonhoeffer Works,* English ed. Vol. 11, *Ecumenical, Academic, and Pastoral Work: 1931–1932.* Edited by Victoria J. Barnett, Mark S. Brocker, and Michael B. Lukens. Translated by Anne Schmidt-Lange, Isabel Best, Nicolas Humphrey, and Marion Pauck. Minneapolis: Fortress Press, 2012.

DBWE 12   Bonhoeffer, Dietrich. *Dietrich Bonhoeffer Works,* English ed. Vol. 12, *Berlin: 1932–1933.* Edited by Larry L. Rasmussen. Translated by Isabel Best and David Higgins. Minneapolis: Fortress Press, 2009.

DBWE 13   Bonhoeffer, Dietrich. *Dietrich Bonhoeffer Works,* English ed. Vol. 13, *London, 1933–1935.* Edited by Keith Clements. Translated by Isabel Best. Minneapolis: Fortress Press, 2007.

DBWE 14   Bonhoeffer, Dietrich. *Dietrich Bonhoeffer Works,* English ed. Vol. 14, *Theological Education at Finkenwalde: 1935–1937.* Edited by H. Gaylon Barker and Mark S. Brocker. Translated by Douglas W. Scott. Minneapolis: Fortress Press, 2013.

DBWE 15   Bonhoeffer, Dietrich. *Dietrich Bonhoeffer Works,* English ed. Vol. 15, *Theological Education Underground: 1937–1940.* Edited by Victoria J. Barnett. Translated by Victoria J. Barnett, Claudia D. Bergmann, Peter Frick, and Scott A. Moore. Minneapolis: Fortress Press, 2012.

NICNT   The New International Commentary on the New Testament

PNTC   The Pillar New Testament Commentary

WBC   Word Biblical Commentary

ZECNT   Zondervan Exegetical Commentary on the New Testament

Notes

Chapter 1

1. *DBWE*, 8:238.
2. *DBWE*, 8:194n1, 195.
3. Dietrich Bonhoeffer and Maria von Wedemeyer, *Love Letters from Cell 92, 1943-1945*, ed. Ruth-Alice von Bismarck and Ulrich Kabitz, trans. John Brownjohn (London: HarperCollins, 1994), 227.
4. "Community, n," OED Online, Oxford University Press, December 2020; accessible via oed.com.
5. "Community, n," OED Online, Oxford University Press, December 2020; accessible via oed.com.
6. John Piper, *Desiring God: Meditations of a Christian Hedonist*, rev. ed. (Colorado Springs, CO: Multnomah, 2011), 10.
7. *DBWE*, 4:99.
8. Robert W. Yarbrough, "Bonhoeffer as Bible Scholar," *Themelios* 37, no. 2 (July 2012): 188.
9. Eberhard Bethge, *Dietrich Bonhoeffer: A Biography*, rev. ed., ed. Victoria J. Barnett (Minneapolis: Fortress, 2000), 3.
10. Bethge, *Dietrich Bonhoeffer*, 20.
11. Bethge, *Dietrich Bonhoeffer*, 3.
12. Charles Marsh, *Strange Glory: A Life of Dietrich Bonhoeffer* (New York: Alfred A. Knopf, 2014), 148.
13. Bethge, *Dietrich Bonhoeffer*, 16–18.
14. Bethge, *Dietrich Bonhoeffer*, 34–36.
15. Bethge, *Dietrich Bonhoeffer*, 38.
16. Sabine Leibholz-Bonhoeffer, *The Bonhoeffers: Portrait of a Family* (London: Sidgwick and Jackson, 1971), 23–24.
17. Marsh, *Strange Glory*, 16–17.
18. Marsh, *Strange Glory*, 17.
19. Ferdinand Schlingensiepen, *Dietrich Bonhoeffer 1906-1945: Martyr, Thinker, Man of Resistance*, trans. Isabel Best (London: T&T Clark, 2010), 16.
20. Schlingensiepen, *Dietrich Bonhoeffer 1906-1945*, 18–19.
21. Bethge, *Dietrich Bonhoeffer*, 81–83.
22. Bethge, *Dietrich Bonhoeffer*, 91–94.
23. Marsh, *Strange Glory*, 69–73.
24. Schlingensiepen, *Dietrich Bonhoeffer 1906-1945*, 57–58.
25. Marsh, *Strange Glory*, 101–3.

26. Schlingensiepen, *Dietrich Bonhoeffer 1906-1945*, 97; Marsh, *Strange Glory*, 140–44.
27. Marsh, *Strange Glory*, 146.
28. *DBWE*, 14:134.
29. Bethge, *Dietrich Bonhoeffer*, 327.
30. Bethge, *Dietrich Bonhoeffer*, 329–31.
31. Schlingensiepen, *Dietrich Bonhoeffer 1906-1945*, 163.
32. Bethge, *Dietrich Bonhoeffer*, 425.
33. Marsh, *Strange Glory*, 260.
34. Schlingensiepen, *Dietrich Bonhoeffer 1906-1945*, 212–13.
35. Bethge, *Dietrich Bonhoeffer*, 623–24.
36. Marsh, *Strange Glory*, 267.
37. Marsh, *Strange Glory*, 275–77.
38. *DBWE*, 15:206.
39. Marsh, *Strange Glory*, 285.
40. Marsh, *Strange Glory*, 289.
41. Marsh, *Strange Glory*, 288.
42. Marsh, *Strange Glory*, 307.
43. Schlingensiepen, *Dietrich Bonhoeffer 1906-1945*, 262.
44. Marsh, *Strange Glory*, 296–97.
45. Schlingensiepen, *Dietrich Bonhoeffer 1906-1945*, 247–48.
46. Marsh, *Strange Glory*, 327.
47. Schlingensiepen, *Dietrich Bonhoeffer 1906-1945*, 309–10.
48. Schlingensiepen, *Dietrich Bonhoeffer 1906-1945*, 314.
49. Schlingensiepen, *Dietrich Bonhoeffer 1906-1945*, 314.
50. Schlingensiepen, *Dietrich Bonhoeffer 1906-1945*, 360.
51. *DBWE*, 8:396. Bonhoeffer was the godfather of Eberhard and Renate's child.
52. Bonhoeffer used a word that could be translated as "psychic" rather than emotional. Emotional makes more sense in the context.

Chapter 2

1. *DBWE*, 14:134.
2. *DBWE*, 14:134.
3. *DBWE*, 5:27.
4. *DBWE*, 5:28.
5. *DBWE*, 5:27–28.
6. *DBWE*, 5:28.
7. *DBWE*, 5:28–29.
8. *DBWE*, 5:29.
9. *DBWE*, 5:29–30.
10. *DBWE*, 5:30.
11. *DBWE*, 5:30–31.
12. *DBWE*, 5:25.
13. Bethge, *Dietrich Bonhoeffer*, 98–99.
14. Marsh, *Strange Glory*, 63–64.
15. Marsh, *Strange Glory*, 75.

16. Marsh, *Strange Glory*, 69–73.
17. Bethge, *Dietrich Bonhoeffer*, 120–21.
18. Bethge, *Dietrich Bonhoeffer*, 328.
19. Bethge, *Dietrich Bonhoeffer*, 327.
20. Schlingensiepen, *Dietrich Bonhoeffer 1906–1945*, 161.
21. Schlingensiepen, *Dietrich Bonhoeffer 1906–1945*, 162.
22. Geffrey B. Kelly, introduction to *DBWE*, 5:12–13.
23. *DBWE*, 13:364.
24. *DBWE*, 4:44.
25. *DBWE*, 14:134.
26. *DBWE*, 13:285.
27. *DBWE*, 4:79.
28. *DBWE*, 4:87.
29. *DBWE*, 14:254.
30. *DBWE*, 14:71.
31. *DBWE*, 14:400.
32. Sarah Hinlicky Wilson, "Ecumenical Dialogues," in *Dictionary of Luther and the Lutheran Traditions*, ed. Timothy J. Wengert (Grand Rapids: Baker Academic, 2017), 206.
33. *DBWE*, 14:71–72.
34. *DBWE*, 5:99.

Chapter 3

1. Bethge, *Dietrich Bonhoeffer*, 56
2. Schlingensiepen, *Dietrich Bonhoeffer 1906–1945*, 18–19.
3. Bethge, *Dietrich Bonhoeffer*, 56–57.
4. Bethge, *Dietrich Bonhoeffer*, 56–58.
5. Bethge, *Dietrich Bonhoeffer*, 59.
6. Bethge, *Dietrich Bonhoeffer*, 65.
7. Bethge, *Dietrich Bonhoeffer*, 77.
8. Bethge, *Dietrich Bonhoeffer*, 66.
9. Marsh, *Strange Glory*, 44.
10. Marsh, *Strange Glory*, 49–50.
11. *DBWE*, 1:1.
12. Bethge, *Dietrich Bonhoeffer*, 81–83.
13. Bethge, *Dietrich Bonhoeffer*, 83.
14. *DBWE*, 1:21.
15. Charles Marsh, *Reclaiming Dietrich Bonhoeffer: The Promise of His Theology* (New York: Oxford University Press, 1994), 68.
16. *DBWE*, 1:7–8.
17. *DBWE*, 1:49.
18. Stephen J. Nichols, *Bonhoeffer on the Christian Life: From the Cross, For the World* (Wheaton, IL: Crossway, 2013), 61.
19. *DBWE*, 1:51.
20. Martin Buber, *I and Thou*, 2nd ed. (New York: Scribner's, 1958), 28.
21. Some scholars debate whether Bonhoeffer did rely on Buber's concepts, but many have made clear that he at least built upon Buber's ideas. See

Clifford J. Green, *Bonhoeffer: A Theology of Sociality*, rev. ed. (Grand Rapids: Eerdmans, 1999), 29–30; and Steven M. Bezner, "Understanding the World Better Than It Understands Itself: The Theological Hermeneutics of Dietrich Bonhoeffer" (PhD diss., Baylor University, 2008), 39n26.

22. *DBWE*, 1:56.
23. *DBWE*, 1:121.
24. *DBWE*, 1:118.
25. *DBWE*, 1:121.
26. John M. Frame, *A History of Western Philosophy and Theology* (Phillipsburg, NJ: P&R, 2015), 270–72.
27. Peter C. Hodgson, "Hegel's Philosophy of Religion," in *The Cambridge Companion to Hegel and Nineteenth-Century Philosophy*, ed. Frederick C. Beiser (Cambridge: Cambridge University Press, 2008), 247.
28. Green, *Bonhoeffer: A Theology of Sociality*, 52n91.
29. Mark Devine, *Bonhoeffer Speaks Today: Following Jesus at All Costs* (Nashville, TN: Broadman & Holman, 2005), 74.
30. Jennifer M. McBride, "Christ Existing as Concrete Community Today," *Theology Today* 71, no. 1 (2014): 92–93.
31. *DBWE*, 5:55.
32. Kelly, *DBWE*, 5:55n20.
33. *DBWE*, 1:146.
34. Andrew Root, *Bonhoeffer as Youth Worker: A Theological Vision for Discipleship and Life Together* (Grand Rapids, MI: Baker Academic, 2014), 43.
35. Root, *Bonhoeffer as Youth Worker*, 43–44n4.
36. *DBWE*, 5:31.
37. Steven D. Paulson, "Christology," in *Dictionary of Luther and the Lutheran Traditions*, ed. Timothy J. Wengert (Grand Rapids: Baker Academic, 2017), 142–45.
38. J. V. Fesko, "Union with Christ," in *Reformation Theology: A Systematic Summary*, ed. Matthew Barrett (Wheaton, IL: Crossway, 2017), 430.
39. *DBWE*, 5:31.
40. Gordon D. Fee, *The First Epistle to the Corinthians*, NICNT (Grand Rapids: Eerdmans, 1987), 33.
41. Fee, *Corinthians*, 45.
42. Thomas R. Schreiner, *Romans*, BECNT (Grand Rapids: Baker Academic, 1998), 428.
43. Clinton E. Arnold, *Ephesians*, ZECNT 10 (Grand Rapids: Zondervan, 2010), 136.
44. Andrew T. Lincoln, *Ephesians*, WBC 42 (Dallas: Word, 1990), 105.
45. I. Howard Marshall, *The Epistles of John*, NICNT (Grand Rapids: Eerdmans, 1978), 111–12.
46. Leon Morris, *The Gospel According to John*, NICNT, rev. ed. (Grand Rapids: Eerdmans, 1995), 650–51.
47. *DBWE*, 5:31–32.
48. To read more on Luther's perspectives on the priesthood of believers, one can reference some of his treatises: *Treatise on the New Testament*

(1520), *To the Christian Nobility of the German Nation Concerning the Reform of the Christian Estate* (1520), or *Concerning the Ministry* (1523).

49. *DBWE*, 11:317.
50. *DBWE*, 5:32–33.
51. *DBWE*, 5:33–34.
52. Matt Boswell and Matt Papa, "How Rich A Treasure We Possess," in *Hymns of Grace* (Los Angeles, CA: The Master's Seminary Press, 2015), 292.
53. *DBWE*, 5:34.

Chapter 4

1. *DBWE*, 10:242.
2. Schlingensiepen, *Dietrich Bonhoeffer 1906–1945*, 58–59.
3. Marsh, *Strange Glory*, 101–3.
4. Marsh, *Strange Glory*, 102.
5. Schlingensiepen, *Dietrich Bonhoeffer 1906–1945*, 63.
6. Schlingensiepen, *Dietrich Bonhoeffer 1906–1945*, 67.
7. Schlingensiepen, *Dietrich Bonhoeffer 1906–1945*, 70.
8. Schlingensiepen, *Dietrich Bonhoeffer 1906–1945*, 65.
9. Bethge, *Dietrich Bonhoeffer*, 151.
10. *DBWE*, 10:315.
11. Schlingensiepen, *Dietrich Bonhoeffer 1906–1945*, 64.
12. N.A. Magnuson, "Social Gospel," in *Evangelical Dictionary of Theology*, 2nd ed., ed. Walter A. Elwell (Grand Rapids, MI: Baker Academic, 2001), 1118–19.
13. Marsh, *Strange Glory*, 104–8.
14. *DBWE*, 10:313.
15. Schlingensiepen, *Dietrich Bonhoeffer 1906–1945*, 69.
16. Schlingensiepen, *Dietrich Bonhoeffer 1906–1945*, 72.
17. Schlingensiepen, *Dietrich Bonhoeffer 1906–1945*, 76–77.
18. *DBWE*, 11:33.
19. Schlingensiepen, *Dietrich Bonhoeffer 1906–1945*, 97.
20. Marsh, *Strange Glory*, 140.
21. Marsh, *Strange Glory*, 144.
22. Bethge, *Dietrich Bonhoeffer*, 173.
23. Marsh, *Strange Glory*, 146.
24. Marsh, *Strange Glory*, 147.
25. *DBWE*, 11:76.
26. Marsh, *Strange Glory*, 147–48.
27. *DBWE*, 14:134.
28. Marsh, *Strange Glory*, 149.
29. Bethge, *Dietrich Bonhoeffer*, 213.
30. *DBWE*, 11:269–71.
31. *DBWE*, 11:292.
32. *DBWE*, 11:296.
33. *DBWE*, 11:297–98.
34. *DBWE*, 11:305.

35. *DBWE*, 11:306.
36. *DBWE*, 11:307.
37. *DBWE*, 12:301.
38. Dane C. Ortlund, "Christocentrism: An Asymmetrical Trinitarianism?" *Themelios* 34, no. 3 (November 2009): 315.
39. *DBWE*, 12:314.
40. Bezner, "Understanding the World," 36.
41. *DBWE*, 12:323.
42. H. Gaylon Barker, *The Cross of Reality: Luther's Theologia Crucis and Bonhoeffer's Christology* (Minneapolis: Fortress, 2015), 240.
43. *DBWE*, 12:325.
44. *DBWE*, 5:35.
45. *DBWE*, 5:35.
46. *DBWE*, 5:35.
47. *DBWE*, 5:35.
48. *DBWE*, 5:36.
49. *DBWE*, 5:35–38.
50. *DBWE*, 5:38.
51. *DBWE*, 5:35.
52. *DBWE*, 5:36.
53. *DBWE*, 5:36.
54. *DBWE*, 5:36.
55. *DBWE*, 5:38.
56. *DBWE*, 5:38.

Chapter 5

1. *DBWE*, 12:69.
2. Rasmussen, *DBWE*, 12:69n1
3. Schlingensiepen, *Dietrich Bonhoeffer 1906–1945*, 104.
4. Bethge, *Dietrich Bonhoeffer*, 174.
5. *DBWE*, 14:134.
6. Bethge, *Dietrich Bonhoeffer*, 215–17.
7. Marsh, *Strange Glory*, 156.
8. Bethge, *Dietrich Bonhoeffer*, 257.
9. Marsh, *Strange Glory*, 158–59.
10. Schlingensiepen, *Dietrich Bonhoeffer 1906–1945*, 117.
11. Marsh, *Strange Glory*, 159.
12. Marsh, *Strange Glory*, 160.
13. Marsh, *Strange Glory*, 161.
14. Victoria Barnett, *For the Soul of the People: Protestant Protest against Hitler* (New York: Oxford University Press, 1992), 30.
15. Barnett, *For the Soul of the People*, 32.
16. Michael B. Lukens, Victoria J. Barnett, and Mark S. Brocker, "Introduction," *DBWE*, 11:2.
17. Barnett, *For the Soul of the People*, 32.
18. Larry L. Rasmussen, "Introduction," *DBWE*, 12:11.
19. Marsh, *Strange Glory*, 162–63.

20. Schlingensiepen, *Dietrich Bonhoeffer 1906–1945*, 125–27.

21. Schlingensiepen, *Dietrich Bonhoeffer 1906–1945*, 127–34.

22. Marsh, *Strange Glory*, 176.

23. Clements, "Introduction," *DBWE*, 13:5.

24. Bethge, *Dietrich Bonhoeffer*, 309–11.

25. Clements, "Introduction," *DBWE*, 13:5–6.

26. *DBWE*, 12:181.

27. *DBWE*, 12:181.

28. Schlingensiepen, *Dietrich Bonhoeffer 1906–1945*, 134–38.

29. Ian Kershaw, *To Hell and Back: Europe, 1914–1949* (New York: Viking, 2015), 214–15.

30. Marsh, *Strange Glory*, 190–91.

31. Bethge, *Dietrich Bonhoeffer*, 327.

32. *DBWE*, 12:184.

33. Carsten Nicolaisen, "Concerning the History of the Bethel Confession," trans. Douglas W. Scott, in *DBWE*, 12:509–10.

34. Nicolaisen, "Concerning the History of the Bethel Confession," in *DBWE*, 12:512–13.

35. *DBWE*, 13:47–49.

36. Bethge, *Dietrich Bonhoeffer*, 303.

37. *DBWE*, 13:47.

38. Nicolaisen, "Concerning the History of the Bethel Confession," in *DBWE*, 12:510.

39. *DBWE*, 12:400.

40. *DBWE*, 12:399.

41. *DBWE*, 5:35.

42. Kelly, *DBWE*, 5:35n12.

43. *DBWE*, 5:38–40.

44. *DBWE*, 5:38.

45. *DBWE*, 5:31.

46. Marsh, *Reclaiming Dietrich Bonhoeffer*, 73.

47. Marsh, *Reclaiming Dietrich Bonhoeffer*, 74.

48. *DBWE*, 5:43–44.

49. *DBWE*, 5:40–43.

50. *DBWE*, 5:45–47.

51. *DBWE*, 5:39.

52. *DBWE*, 5:42.

53. *DBWE*, 5:42.

54. *DBWE*, 5:42.

55. *DBWE*, 5:43.

56. *DBWE*, 5:42.

57. *DBWE*, 5:44.

58. *DBWE*, 5:44.

59. *DBWE*, 5:43.

60. *DBWE*, 5:43.

61. *DBWE*, 5:45.

62. *DBWE*, 5:46.

63. *DBWE*, 5:47.

64. *DBWE*, 5:93.
65. *DBWE*, 5:93–94.
66. *DBWE*, 5:94–95.
67. *DBWE*, 5:95.
68. *DBWE*, 5:96.
69. *DBWE*, 5:97.
70. *DBWE*, 5:97.
71. *DBWE*, 5:98–99.
72. *DBWE*, 5:99.
73. *DBWE*, 5:99.
74. *DBWE*, 5:100–101.
75. *DBWE*, 5:101–3.
76. *DBWE*, 5:103–7.
77. *DBWE*, 5:95.
78. *DBWE*, 5:95.
79. *DBWE*, 5:96.
80. Thomas à Kempis, *The Imitation of Christ*, trans. William C. Creasy (Macon, GA: Mercer University Press, 2007), 17.
81. Nichols, *Bonhoeffer on the Christian Life*, 73.
82. Stephen J. Nichols, personal correspondence, March 6, 2018.
83. Martin Luther, *The Annotated Luther*, vol. 1, *The Roots of Reform*, ed. Timothy J. Wengert (Minneapolis: Fortress, 2015), 522–23.
84. *DBWE*, 5:94.
85. Nichols, *Bonhoeffer on the Christian Life*, 73.

Chapter 6

1. *DBWE*, 15:172–73.
2. Schlingensiepen, *Dietrich Bonhoeffer 1906–1945*, 180.
3. Marsh, *Strange Glory*, 332–33.
4. Marsh, *Strange Glory*, 230.
5. Schlingensiepen, *Dietrich Bonhoeffer 1906–1945*, 177.
6. Bethge, *Dietrich Bonhoeffer*, 425.
7. Marsh, *Strange Glory*, 231–34.
8. Marsh, *Strange Glory*, 260.
9. Marsh, *Strange Glory*, 247.
10. Bethge, *Dietrich Bonhoeffer*, 451.
11. Bethge, *Dietrich Bonhoeffer*, 462–63.
12. Kelly, "Introduction," *DBWE*, 5:10.
13. *DBWE*, 11:271–72.
14. Kelly, "Introduction," *DBWE*, 5:11.
15. Kelly, "Introduction," *DBWE*, 5:11.
16. Bethge, *Dietrich Bonhoeffer*, 466.
17. *DBWE*, 14:95.
18. Bethge, *Dietrich Bonhoeffer*, 466–68.
19. Marsh, *Strange Glory*, 234.
20. Paul R. House, *Bonhoeffer's Seminary Vision: A Case for Costly Discipleship and Life Together* (Wheaton, IL: Crossway, 2015), 137.

21. *DBWE*, 15:20.
22. Kelly, "Introduction," *DBWE*, 5:3.
23. *DBWE*, 15:72.
24. Kelly, "Introduction," *DBWE*, 5:4.
25. Kelly, "Introduction," *DBWE*, 5:6.
26. Schlingensiepen, *Dietrich Bonhoeffer 1906–1945*, 210–11.
27. Schlingensiepen, *Dietrich Bonhoeffer 1906–1945*, 212–13.
28. *DBWE*, 5:48.
29. Augustine, *The Augustine Series*, vol. 4, *The Monastic Rule*, ed. Boniface Ramsey, trans. Agatha Mary and Gerald Bonner (Hyde Park, NY: New City, 2004), 106.
30. Augustine, *The Augustine Series*, vol. 4, *The Monastic Rule*, 112.
31. *DBWE*, 5:49.
32. *DBWE*, 5:53.
33. *DBWE*, 5:53.
34. *DBWE*, 5:157.
35. *DBWE*, 5:55.
36. *DBWE*, 5:55.
37. *DBWE*, 5:56–57.
38. *DBWE*, 5:57–58.
39. *DBWE*, 5:58.
40. *DBWE*, 5:59.
41. *DBWE*, 5:60.
42. *DBWE*, 5:61.
43. *DBWE*, 5:61.
44. *DBWE*, 5:62.
45. *DBWE*, 5:63.
46. *DBWE*, 5:63–64.
47. *DBWE*, 5:65.
48. *DBWE*, 5:66.
49. Bethge, *Dietrich Bonhoeffer*, 24–25.
50. *DBWE*, 5:67–68.
51. *DBWE*, 5:68.
52. *DBWE*, 5:68–69.
53. *DBWE*, 5:69–70.
54. *DBWE*, 5:70.
55. *DBWE*, 5:71.
56. *DBWE*, 5:72.
57. *DBWE*, 5:72.
58. *DBWE*, 5:72–73.
59. *DBWE*, 5:73–74.
60. *DBWE*, 5:75–76.
61. *DBWE*, 5:76.
62. *DBWE*, 5:75–76. For further background on Bonhoeffer's use of the "I-Thou" relationship see Buber, *I and Thou*, 54, 62–63.
63. *DBWE*, 5:76–80.
64. William Macleod, "Bonhoeffer—A Reliable Guide?" *Free Church Witness* (September 2016), 4.

65. Macleod, "Bonhoeffer, A Reliable Guide?," 4.

66. *DBWE*, 5:60.

67. *DBWE*, 5:51, 55, 64, 72, 77.

68. According to *DBWE*, 5:186–88, Bonhoeffer cited from the following hymnals in *Life Together*: *Evangelisches Gesangbuch für Brandenburg und Pommern* (Berlin/Frankfurt, 1931) and Otto Riethmüller, ed. *Ein neues Lied* (Berlin-Dahlem, 1932).

69. Catherine Winkworth, preface to *Lyra Germanica*, 2nd series, *The Christian Life* (New York: Anson D.F. Randolph, 1859), v–xii.

70. Johann Heermann, "Christ Our Champion," in *Lyra Germanica*, 64–65.

71. Heermann, "Christ Our Champion," in *Lyra Germanica*, 64–65.

72. *DBWE*, 5:48.

73. *DBWE*, 5:49–50.

74. Bethge, *Dietrich Bonhoeffer*, 35.

75. James K.A. Smith, *Cultural Liturgies*, vol. 1, *Desiring the Kingdom: Worship, Worldview, and Cultural Formation* (Grand Rapids: Baker Academic, 2009), 25.

76. *DBWE* 12:472–76.

77. *DBWE*, 15:505.

Chapter 7

1. *DBWE*, 5:118.

2. *DBWE* 3:96.

3. *DBWE* 5:15.

4. Donald S. Whitney, *Spiritual Disciplines for the Christian Life*, rev. ed. (Colorado Springs, CO: NavPress, 2014), 7.

5. *DBWE*, 5:22.

6. Schlingensiepen, *Dietrich Bonhoeffer 1906-1945*, 314.

7. Schlingensiepen, *Dietrich Bonhoeffer 1906-1945*, 360.

8. Marsh, *Strange Glory*, 388.

9. Marsh, *Strange Glory*, 390.

10. Schlingensiepen, *Dietrich Bonhoeffer 1906-1945*, 377.

11. Bethge, *Dietrich Bonhoeffer*, 924.

12. Marsh, *Strange Glory*, 393–94.

13. Bethge, *Dietrich Bonhoeffer*, 930–31.

14. Schlingensiepen, *Dietrich Bonhoeffer 1906-1945*, 379.

15. Schlingensiepen, *Dietrich Bonhoeffer 1906-1945*, 378.

Works Cited

À Kempis, Thomas. *The Imitation of Christ*. Translated by William C. Creasy. Macon, GA: Mercer University Press, 2007.

Arnold, Clinton E. *Ephesians*, ZECNT 10. Grand Rapids: Zondervan, 2010.

Augustine, *The Augustine Series*. Vol. 4, *The Monastic Rule*. Edited by Boniface Ramsey. Translated by Agatha Mary and Gerald Bonner. Hyde Park, NY: New City Press, 2004.

Barker, H. Gaylon. *The Cross of Reality: Luther's Theologia Crucis and Bonhoeffer's Christology*. Minneapolis: Fortress Press, 2015.

Barnett, Victoria. *For the Soul of the People: Protestant Protest against Hitler*. New York: Oxford University Press, 1992.

Bonhoeffer, Dietrich and Maria von Wedemeyer. *Love Letters from Cell 92, 1943–1945*. Edited by Ruth-Alice von Bismarck and Ulrich Kabitz. Translated by John Brownjohn. London, HarperCollins, 1994.

Bethge, Eberhard. *Dietrich Bonhoeffer: A Biography*. Rev. ed. Edited by Victoria J. Barnett. Minneapolis: Fortress Press, 2000.

Bezner, Steven M. "Understanding the World Better Than It Understands Itself: The Theological Hermeneutics of Dietrich Bonhoeffer." PhD diss., Baylor University, 2008.

Boswell, Matt, and Matt Papa. "How Rich A Treasure We Possess." In *Hymns of Grace*. Los Angeles, CA: The Master's Seminary Press, 2015.

Buber, Martin. *I and Thou*, 2nd ed. New York: Charles Scribner's Sons, 1958.

Devine, Mark. *Bonhoeffer Speaks Today: Following Jesus at All Costs*. Nashville, TN: Broadman & Holman Publishers, 2005.

Fee, Gordon D. *The First Epistle to the Corinthians*, NICNT. Grand Rapids: Eerdmans, 1987.

Fesko, J. V. "Union with Christ." In *Reformation Theology: A Systematic Summary*. Edited by Matthew Barrett. Wheaton, IL: Crossway, 2017.

Frame, John M. *A History of Western Philosophy and Theology*. Phillipsburg, NJ: P&R Publishing, 2015.

Green, Clifford J. *Bonhoeffer: A Theology of Sociality*. Rev. ed. Grand Rapids: Eerdmans, 1999.

Hodgson, Peter C. "Hegel's Philosophy of Religion." In *The Cambridge Companion to Hegel and Nineteenth-Century Philosophy*. Edited by Frederick C. Beiser. Cambridge: Cambridge University Press, 2008.

House, Paul R. *Bonhoeffer's Seminary Vision: A Case for Costly Discipleship and Life Together*. Wheaton, IL: Crossway, 2015.

Kershaw, Ian. *To Hell and Back: Europe, 1914–1949*. New York: Viking, 2015.

Lincoln, Andrew T. *Ephesians*, WBC 42. Dallas: Word Books, 1990.

Leibholz-Bonhoeffer, Sabine. *The Bonhoeffers: Portrait of a Family*. London: Sidgwick and Jackson, 1971.

Luther, Martin. *The Annotated Luther*. Vol. 1, *The Roots of Reform*. Edited by Timothy J. Wengert. Minneapolis: Fortress Press, 2015.

Macleod, William. "Bonhoeffer—A Reliable Guide?" *Free Church Witness* (September 2016): 3–6.

Magnuson, N.A. "Social Gospel." In *Evangelical Dictionary of Theology*. 2nd ed. Edited by Walter A. Elwell. Grand Rapids, MI: Baker Academic, 2001.

Marshall, I. Howard. *The Epistles of John*, NICNT. Grand Rapids: Eerdmans, 1978.

Marsh, Charles. *Reclaiming Dietrich Bonhoeffer: The Promise of His Theology*. New York: Oxford University Press, 1994.

———. *Strange Glory: A Life of Dietrich Bonhoeffer*. New York: Alfred A. Knopf, 2014.

McBride, Jennifer M. "Christ Existing as Concrete Community Today." *Theology Today* 71, no. 1 (2014):92–105.

Morris, Leon. *The Gospel According to John*, NICNT. Rev. ed. Grand Rapids: Eerdmans, 1995.

Nicolaisen, Carsten. "Concerning the History of the Bethel Confession." Translated by Douglas W. Scott. In *DBWE*, 12:509–13.

Nichols, Stephen J. *Bonhoeffer on the Christian Life: From the Cross, For the World*. Wheaton, IL: Crossway, 2013.

———. Personal Correspondence, March 6, 2018.

Oxford English Dictionary, s.v. "Community," accessed December 27, 2020, https://www-oed-com.ezproxy.sbts.edu/view/Entry/37337?redirectedFrom=community#eid.

Paulson, Steven D. "Christology." In *Dictionary of Luther and the Lutheran Traditions*. Edited by Timothy J. Wengert. Grand Rapids: Baker Academic, 2017.

Piper, John. *Desiring God: Meditations of a Christian Hedonist*. Rev. ed. Colorado Springs, CO: Multnomah Books, 2011.

Root, Andrew. *Bonhoeffer as Youth Worker: A Theological Vision for Discipleship and Life Together*. Grand Rapids, MI: Baker Academic, 2014.

Schlingensiepen, Ferdinand. *Dietrich Bonhoeffer 1906–1945: Martyr, Thinker, Man of Resistance*. Translated by Isabel Best. London: T&T Clark, 2010.

Schreiner, Thomas R. *Romans*, BECNT. Grand Rapids: Baker Academic, 1998.

Smith, James K.A. Cultural Liturgies. Vol. 1, *Desiring the Kingdom: Worship, Worldview, and Cultural Formation*. Grand Rapids: Baker Academic, 2009.

Whitney, Donald S. *Spiritual Disciplines for the Christian Life*. Rev. ed. Colorado Springs, CO: NavPress, 2014.

Wilson, Sarah Hinlicky. "Ecumenical Dialogues." In *Dictionary of Luther and the Lutheran Traditions*. Edited by Timothy J. Wengert. Grand Rapids: Baker Academic, 2017.

Winkworth, Catherine, trans. *Lyra Germanica*. 2nd series. *The Christian Life*. New York: Anson D.F. Randolph, 1859.

Yarbrough, Robert W. "Bonhoeffer as Bible Scholar." *Themelios* 37, no. 2 (July 2012): 185–90.

Subject Index

Scripture Index

Old Testament

New Testament

LEARN TO LIVE THEOLOGY ON THE SHOULDERS OF GIANTS

The *Lived Theology* series explores aspects of Christian doctrine through the eyes of the men and women who practiced it.

To learn more and order, visit LexhamPress.com